Microsoft® Excel

Version 3

Written, edited, and produced by Microsoft Corporation

Distributed by Microsoft Press

Step by Step

PUBLISHED BY
Microsoft Press
A Division of Microsoft Corporation
One Microsoft Way, Redmond, Washington 98052-6399

Library of Congress Cataloging-in-Publication Data
Microsoft Excel step-by-step: Apple Macintosh version / Microsoft
    Corporation.
        p.   cm.
    Includes index.
    ISBN 1-55615-318-X
    1. Microsoft Excel (Computer program)   2. Macintosh (Computer)-
-Programming.   3. Business--Computer programs.   I. Microsoft.
HF5548.4.M523M535   1991
650' .0285'5369--dc20   91-2322
                                                         CIP

Printed and bound in the United States of America.

 2 3 4 5 6 7 8 9 MLML 6 5 4 3 2 1

Distributed to the book trade in Canada by Macmillan of Canada, a division of Canada Publishing Corporation.

Distributed to the book trade outside the United States and Canada by Penguin Books Ltd.

Penguin Books Ltd., Harmondsworth, Middlesex, England
Penguin Books Australia Ltd., Ringwood, Victoria, Australia
Penguin Books N.Z. Ltd., 182-190 Wairau Road, Auckland 10, New Zealand

British Cataloging-in-Publication Data available

All names of companies, products, street addresses, and persons contained herein are part of a completely fictitious scenario or scenarios, and are designed solely to document the use of a Microsoft product.

Microsoft, MS, and PowerPoint are registered trademarks of Microsoft Corporation.
OS/2 and Operating System/2 are registered trademarks licensed to Microsoft Corporation.
Apple, AppleTalk, HyperCard, ImageWriter, LaserWriter, Macintosh, and MultiFinder are registered trademarks and Finder is a trademark of Apple Computer, Incorporated.
Dow Jones is a registered trademark of Dow Jones and Company, Incorporated.
Lotus and 1-2-3 are registered trademarks of Lotus Development Corporation.

Microsoft documentation uses the term "OS/2" to refer to the OS/2 systems—Microsoft® Operating System/2® (MS® OS/2®) and IBM® OS/2®. Similarly, the term "DOS" refers to the Microsoft® MS-DOS® and IBM Personal Computer DOS operating systems. The name of a specific operating system is used when it is necessary to note features that are unique to that system.

This book was produced using Microsoft Word.

Document Number ABSTEP-0991

Contents

About This Book

You'll find Microsoft® Excel to be a powerful spreadsheet application for analyzing and charting your data and creating effective presentations. *Microsoft Excel Step by Step* is a comprehensive tutorial that shows you how to use Microsoft Excel for many common tasks. Although *Microsoft Excel Step by Step* can be used in a classroom, you can also use this book as a tutorial to learn Microsoft Excel at your own pace and at your own convenience.

Using This Book for Self-Paced Learning

This book can be used by new users learning Microsoft Excel for the first time, or by experienced users who want to learn to use the new features in Microsoft Excel version 3.0. Whether you're a novice or an experienced user, *Microsoft Excel Step by Step* will help you to get the most out of Microsoft Excel.

If you are	Start here
New to the Apple Macintosh	Lesson 1, "Getting Started with Microsoft Excel"
Familiar with a graphical computer environment, but are new to Microsoft Excel	Lesson 2, "Creating a Worksheet"
Experienced with Microsoft Excel	Appendix B, "New Features of Microsoft Excel Version 3.0"

The modular design of this book allows you to go through the lessons in any order, skip lessons, and repeat lessons later to brush up on certain skills. You start each lesson by opening a practice file from the disk. You then rename the practice file so that the original file remains unchanged while you work on your own version. You don't need to complete a lesson in order to go through the next one. If you make a mistake in your file, you can just start that lesson over.

Using This Book as a Classroom Aid

If you're an instructor, you can use *Microsoft Excel Step by Step* for teaching Microsoft Excel to novice users, and for teaching the new features of Microsoft Excel version 3.0 to experienced users. You may want to select certain lessons that meet your students' needs and incorporate your own demonstrations into the lessons.

If you plan to teach the entire contents of this book, you should probably set aside three full days of classroom time to allow for discussion, questions, and any customized practice you may create.

Using the Practice Files

Inside this book you'll find a disk named "Microsoft Excel Step by Step Practice Files." Copy the Practice folder with all its files to the Microsoft Excel folder on your hard disk.

Copy the practice files

1 Insert the Practice Files disk into the disk drive on your Macintosh.

2 Double-click the Practice Files disk icon to display the contents of the disk.

3 Drag the Practice folder to your Microsoft Excel folder on your hard disk.

4 Eject the Practice Files disk by dragging it to the Trash.

If you need help with this procedure, see your Macintosh documentation.

With the practice files you can start the tutorial at any lesson, or go through the lessons in any order you want. As you go through each lesson, make sure to follow the instructions for renaming the practice files so that you can review the lesson later with a fresh practice file.

For a complete list of practice files and the lessons in which they are used, see "List of Practice Files," later in this introduction.

Conventions Used in This Book

Notational Conventions

- Characters you type appear in **bold.**
- Important terms and titles of books appear in *italic.*

Procedural Conventions

- Procedures you are to follow are given in numbered lists (1, 2, ...).
  A triangular bullet (▶) indicates a procedure with only one step.
- Numbered steps are generic or mouse-specific. If a numbered step is mouse-specific, it is followed by an alternative keyboard step, marked with a key icon (⌨).
- Commands are described with the menu name preceding the command name. For example, if you need to choose the Open command from the File menu, the lesson will tell you to "Choose File Open."
- The word *choose* is used for carrying out a command.
- The word *select* is used for highlighting cells, text, and menu or command names, and for selecting options in a dialog box.

Mouse Conventions

- *Point* means to move the mouse pointer to an object on the screen. For example, "Point to cell A1."
- *Click* means to point to an object and then press and release the mouse button. For example, "Click cell A1."
- *Drag* means to press and hold the mouse button while you move the mouse. For example, "Drag from cell A1 to cell B5."
- *Double-click* means to rapidly press and release the mouse button twice. For example, "Double-click the Microsoft Excel icon to start Microsoft Excel."

Keyboard Conventions

- Names of keys are in small capital letters; for example, TAB and SHIFT.

- You can use the ENTER and RETURN keys interchangeably, unless specifically noted.

- If you use the RETURN key to enter text and carry out commands, you should choose the Options Workspace command and turn off the Move Selection After Return check box. Otherwise, the wrong cell will be active after certain procedures.

- The COMMAND key is the key marked with a ⌘ symbol.

- You can choose commands with the keyboard by pressing the SLASH (/) key or the PERIOD key on the numeric keypad followed by the keys for the underlined letters in the menu name and command name. For some commands, you can press the COMMAND key combination listed in the menu. These shortcut keys are given in parentheses after the procedure.

- The letters you press to choose a command from a menu are underlined in procedures the same way they are underlined on the screen. For example, "Choose File Open" means that you can press the SLASH key, then the F and O keys to choose the File Open command.

- A plus sign (+) between two key names means that you must press those keys at the same time. For example, "Press SHIFT+SPACEBAR" means that you hold down the SHIFT key while you press the SPACEBAR.

- A comma (,) between two key names means that you must press those keys sequentially. For example, "Press SLASH, F, O" means that you first press and release the SLASH key, then the F key, and then the O key.

Other Features of This Book

- Text in the left margin summarizes main points, or gives tips or additional useful information.

- You'll find optional "You Try It" exercises at the end of most lessons. These exercises are less structured than the lessons to help you practice what you learned in the lesson.

Microsoft Excel Documentation

Using *Microsoft Excel Step by Step* will help you learn about your Microsoft Excel documentation. You'll find references to the *Microsoft Excel User's Guide*, online Help, and the *Microsoft Excel Function Reference* throughout this book. Using the references to these sources will help you to make greater use of Microsoft Excel's powerful features.

Microsoft Excel User's Guide

The *User's Guide* is divided into parts according to the types of Microsoft Excel documents and the tasks you want to perform, such as automating your work and writing macros. Each chapter describes a particular task and explains the procedures you follow to accomplish that task.

Microsoft Excel Function Reference

The *Function Reference* is an alphabetic listing of all worksheet and macro sheet functions. The function topics include descriptions of arguments, notes, examples, and lists of related functions.

Online Help

You can get Help on your screen by pressing COMMAND+SLASH (/) or HELP if you have an extended keyboard. If you have a question about a specific screen region, command, or dialog box, you can press COMMAND+SHIFT+QUESTION MARK, SHIFT+F1, or SHIFT+HELP to get context-sensitive Help. Using the Microsoft Excel macro language, you can also develop your own custom help.

Microsoft Excel Tutorial

The online Tutorial provides overviews and hands-on practice for each of the main parts of Microsoft Excel. To start the Tutorial, double-click the Microsoft Excel Tutorial icon in the Microsoft Excel folder.

Other References

For more information on Microsoft Excel, spreadsheet design, or the presentation of data, see the bibliography in Appendix C, "For More Information."

List of Practice Files

You will find the practice files on the Microsoft Excel Step by Step Practice File disk included with this book. Be sure to copy the entire Practice folder to your hard disk. The following files are in the Practice folder:

ARRAYS08	LESSON06A	PRINTER ART16
CAMPAIGN02	LESSON06B	SALARY13 CHART
CAMPAIGN03	LESSON06C	SALARY14 CHART
CAMPAIGN03A	LESSON06D	SALES CHART15 TEMPLATE
CAMPAIGN04	LESSON07	
CAMPAIGN04A	LESSON07 WORKSPACE	SALES CHART16 TEMPLATE
CAMPAIGN05		SALES CHART17 TEMPLATE
CONSULT05	LESSON08 MACROS	
COPIER07	LESSON08 WORKSPACE	SALES HISTORY17
COPY RECORDS11	LESSON10	SALES17 MACROS
CUSTOM FUNCTION08 MACROS	LESSON11	SALES REPORT07
	LESSON11 WORKSPACE	SOUTH07
CUSTOM FUNCTION08 WORKSHEET	LESSON12	UTRYIT05 WORKSPACE
	LESSON13	UTRYIT07 WORKSPACE
EMPLOYEE13 CHART	LESSON14	UTRYIT11
FAX07	LESSON14 CHART	UTRYIT13
GOAL SEEK08	LESSON14 WORKSPACE	UTRYIT14
IF_FUNCTION08	LESSON15 WORKSPACE	UTRYIT14 CHART
INTRODUCTION08		UTRYIT14 WORKSPACE
LESSON02	LESSON15A	
LESSON03	LESSON15B	UTRYIT17 WORKSPACE
LESSON04	LESSON16	
LESSON05A	LESSON17	WCS DEPARTMENTS07
LESSON05B	NORTH07	
LESSON06 WORKSPACE	PRINTER07	

The following table lists the practice files you will use in each lesson. The name you will use to rename the practice file appears in the last column. Some files are used as sample solutions to compare with your results at the end of a lesson. Other files are for demonstration purposes only.

In this lesson	Open this file	To create or review this document
Lesson 1, "Getting Started with Microsoft Excel"	Worksheet1 Worksheet2 (blank worksheets)	
Lesson 2, "Creating a Worksheet"	LESSON02	BUDGET
	Worksheet1 (blank worksheet)	CAMPAIGN
	CAMPAIGN02	
Lesson 3, "Formatting a Worksheet"	LESSON03	BUDGET
	CAMPAIGN03	CAMPAIGN
	CAMPAIGN03A	
Lesson 4, "Copying and Moving Cell Data and Formats"	LESSON04	BUDGET
	CAMPAIGN04	CAMPAIGN
	CAMPAIGN04A	
Lesson 5, "Linking Worksheets"	LESSON05A	BUDGET
	LESSON05B	SALES HISTORY
	UTRYIT05 WORKSPACE	BUDGET WORKSPACE
	CAMPAIGN05	
	CONSULT05	
Lesson 6, "Using Names on a Worksheet"	LESSON06 WORKSPACE	
	LESSON06A	BUDGET
	LESSON06B	SALES HISTORY
	LESSON06C	BUDGET
	LESSON06D	

In this lesson	Open this file	To create or review this document
Lesson 7, "Worksheet Outlining and Data Consolidation"	LESSON07	WCS DIVISIONS
	LESSON07 WORKSPACE	
	COPIER07	COPIER
	FAX07	FAX
	PRINTER07	PRINTER
	WCS DEPARTMENTS07	WCS DEPARTMENTS
	UTRYIT07 WORKSPACE	
	NORTH07	NORTH
	SOUTH07	SOUTH
	SALES REPORT07	SALES REPORT
Lesson 8, "Advanced Worksheet Features"	LESSON08 WORKSPACE	
	INTRODUCTION08	
	ARRAYS08	
	GOAL SEEK08	
	IF_FUNCTION08	
	CUSTOM FUNCTION08 MACROS	
	CUSTOM FUNCTION08 WORKSHEET	
	LESSON08 MACROS	
Lesson 9, "Installing and Setting Up Your Printer"	No file	
Lesson 10, "Setting Up the Page and Printing"	LESSON10	BUDGET
Lesson 11, "Setting Up a Database on Your Worksheet"	LESSON11 WORKSPACE	
	LESSON11	PERSONNEL
	COPY RECORDS11	
	UTRYIT11	PRINTER DIV. PERSONNEL

In this lesson	Open this file	To create or review this document
Lesson 12, "Extracting and Analyzing Data in a Database"	LESSON12	WCS PERSONNEL
Lesson 13, "Creating a Chart"	LESSON13	SALES HISTORY SALES CHART LESSON13 WORKSPACE
	UTRYIT13	SALARY CHART EMPLOYEE CHART
	SALARY13 CHART	
	EMPLOYEE13 CHART	
Lesson 14, "Formatting a Chart"	LESSON14 WORKSPACE	
	LESSON14	SALES HISTORY
	LESSON14 CHART	SALES CHART SALES CHART TEMPLATE
	UTRYIT14 WORKSPACE	
	UTRYIT14	
	UTRYIT14 CHART	SALARY CHART
	SALARY14 CHART	
Lesson 15, "Editing Chart Data Series"	LESSON15 WORKSPACE	
	LESSON15A	SALES HISTORY
	LESSON15B	STOCK STOCKXY
	SALES CHART15 TEMPLATE	SALES CHART STOCK CHART
Lesson 16, "Using Embedded Charts and Worksheet Graphics"	LESSON16	PRESENTATION
	SALES CHART16 TEMPLATE	PRINTER CHART
	PRINTER ART16	

In this lesson	Open this file	To create or review this document
Lesson 17, "Recording Macros"	LESSON17	WCS SALES
	Macro1 (blank macro sheet)	SALES MACROS
	SALES CHART17 TEMPLATE	
	UTRYIT17 WORKSPACE	
	SALES HISTORY17	
	SALES17 MACROS	

1 Microsoft Excel Basics

Getting Started with Microsoft Excel

You will learn to:

- Start and end a Microsoft Excel session.
- Work with windows.
- Choose commands from menus.
- Select options in dialog boxes.
- Create a new document.
- Get Help.

Estimated lesson time: 30 minutes

This lesson teaches you the basic features of Microsoft Excel version 3.0.

Microsoft Excel is a spreadsheet application used to calculate, update, and present data. You can use Microsoft Excel to help you with your work in many ways. For example, you can create budgets, track sales, and update financial information. You can automate your tasks with macros and create high-quality presentations.

Your work is stored in documents such as worksheets, charts, macro sheets, and templates. The documents you create are displayed on your screen in windows that you can move and resize.

In this lesson, you'll work with windows and learn about the types of documents used in Microsoft Excel. You'll choose commands from menus and select options in dialog boxes. You'll open and close worksheets and get online Help.

Starting Microsoft Excel

This lesson includes basic Apple Macintosh procedures. If you are unfamiliar with the Macintosh, you can learn to use it as you learn Microsoft Excel. For more information on the Macintosh, see your Macintosh documentation.

You start Microsoft Excel by choosing its icon. The Microsoft Excel icon looks like this:

You can also start Microsoft Excel by choosing one of the document icons. Microsoft Excel has five types of documents: worksheets, charts, macro sheets, workspace files, and templates. The Microsoft Excel document icons look like this:

Worksheet   Chart   Macro sheet   Workspace   Sheet template

Start Microsoft Excel

In many of the procedures, it is assumed that you are using a mouse; however, you can also perform these procedures with the keyboard. A step marked by a key icon (⊘) is a keyboard alternative to the preceding mouse step.

▶ Double-click the Microsoft Excel icon.

Each time you start Microsoft Excel, it opens a new worksheet.

The worksheet window   When you start Microsoft Excel, it opens a new worksheet called Worksheet1. The next worksheet you create is called Worksheet2, and so on. You can rename a document when you save it. Each worksheet is displayed in a window. For an overview of the Microsoft Excel worksheet window, see the online Tutorial.

The worksheet window looks like this:

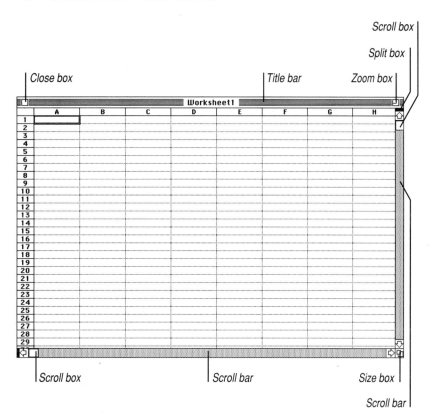

Scroll box |

Split box |

Close box   Title bar   Zoom box |

Scroll box | Scroll bar | Size box |

Scroll bar |

Run the Tutorial (optional)

1 Go back to the Finder. If you are running MultiFinder, click the Microsoft Excel icon in the upper-right corner of your screen. Otherwise, you will have to quit Microsoft Excel.

2 Double-click the Tutorial icon.

3 Click Introduction.

4 Click Tour of the Screen.

5 Follow the instructions on the screen.

6 To quit the tutorial, click the question mark icon in the lower-right corner and click Quit.

Using the mouse   There are three basic mouse actions: click, double-click, and drag. To click an object on the screen, point to it with the mouse pointer and rapidly press and release the mouse button. To double-click an object, press and release the mouse button twice in rapid succession. To drag, point to an object with the mouse pointer, press and hold the mouse button, drag the mouse until the pointer is in the position you want, and release the mouse button.

Controlling a window with the mouse   You can scroll through, size, move, split, and close a window by using the mouse.

To	Do this
Scroll through a window (to see another part of the document)	Click the scroll bars or drag the scroll box.
Change the size of a window	Drag the size box.
Enlarge a window to fill the screen	Click the zoom box or double-click the title bar.
Restore a window to its original size	Click the zoom box or double-click the title bar.
Move a window	Drag the title bar.
Split a window	Drag the split box on the scroll bar to where you want the split.
Close a window	Click the close box.

The mouse pointer   When you use the mouse to point to various parts of the window, the mouse pointer changes shape to perform different tasks. Try moving the mouse pointer around on the screen to see how it changes shape.

This pointer appears	When you point to
▶	The menu bar to choose a command or the borders of a window (title bar and scroll bars).
I	Text in the formula bar you want to edit.
⊕	A cell on the worksheet.
┼┼ ┼	A column heading or row heading boundary to change column width or row height.
┤├ ≑	A split box on the scroll bar to split a window vertically or horizontally.
⬤	A button on a worksheet or a term in a Help topic that you can click to go to another topic.

Scrolling Through a Document Window

When a document is too large to fit within a window, you can scroll through the document window to see other parts of the document.

Scroll through the document

You can scroll through the window with the mouse in three ways: click the scroll arrow, drag the scroll box, or click anywhere above or below the scroll box. As you scroll, the scroll box moves to indicate your position in the document.

1   Click the down scroll arrow.

   The window moves down one line.

2   Drag the scroll box down to the bottom of the scroll bar.

   The window moves down to display the end of the worksheet.

3   Click the scroll bar above the scroll box.

   The worksheet moves up one window.

You can also scroll with the keyboard. You'll learn how in Lesson 2, "Creating a Worksheet."

Understanding Menus

The menu bar contains menus, and the menus contain commands. In this section you will use commands to create and work with new document windows.

Microsoft Excel menu bars change to suit the type of document you're working with.

Microsoft Excel menu bars In Microsoft Excel, the menu bars change slightly depending on what type of document you're working on. For example, when a chart is the active document, the menu bar contains a Chart menu and a Gallery menu.

When you select a menu, it displays a list of commands.

⧭ File	**Edit**	Formula	Format	Data	Options	Macro	Window

```
Can't Undo      ⌘Z
Can't Repeat    ⌘Y

Cut             ⌘H
Copy            ⌘C
Paste           ⌘U
Clear...        ⌘B
Paste Special...
Paste Link

Delete...       ⌘K
Insert...       ⌘I

Fill Right      ⌘R
Fill Down       ⌘D
Fill Workgroup...
```

Characteristics of commands As you use the commands on the menus, you'll notice that some commands list shortcut key combinations to the right of the command name. After you become familiar with the menus and commands, these shortcut keys can save you time.

Microsoft Excel commands that are unavailable appear dimmed.

When a command name appears dimmed, it doesn't apply to your current situation or is unavailable. For example, the Paste command appears dimmed if the Copy or Cut command has not been used first.

When a command name has a check mark, the command is already in effect. For example, when you display the Window menu, a check mark appears next to the name of the active window.

When you choose a command name followed by an ellipsis (...), Microsoft Excel displays a dialog box so that you can provide more information. The dialog box prompts you to enter information or lists alternatives you can select from. For example, on the File menu the Open command is followed by an ellipsis, because you need to tell Microsoft Excel which document you want to open. When you choose this command, a dialog box prompts you for the filename.

How commands are named   In this book, commands are described by the menu name followed by the command name. For example, the Short Menus command on the Options menu is called the Options Short Menus command.

The Options Short Menus and Options Full Menus commands   You can use short menus or full menus in Microsoft Excel. Short menus display only the most frequently used commands. Full menus display all commands. When you start Microsoft Excel, full menus are displayed. You can switch to short menus by using the Options Short Menus command. You can switch back again by choosing the Options Full Menus command.

Choosing Menu Commands

Choosing a command with the mouse   To choose a command with the mouse, point to the menu name and drag to the command you want. To cancel a menu without choosing a command, move the pointer away from the menu and then release the mouse button.

Choosing a command with the keyboard   To display a menu, press the SLASH (/) key or the PERIOD key on the numeric keypad to activate the menu bar, and then press the key for the underlined letter in the menu you want. To choose a command, press the key for the underlined letter in the command you want. For example, to choose the Open command from the File menu, press SLASH, F, O. Or you can use the ARROW keys to move between menus and commands, and press ENTER to choose the menu or command you want. To cancel a menu without choosing a command, press COMMAND+PERIOD or ESC. You can also carry out some commands with the keyboard shortcuts listed in the menu.

If the underlines don't appear in the menu names when you press the SLASH key, choose the Options Workspace command and select the On option under Command Underlines.

If you want to use the PERIOD key on the numeric keypad to choose commands, make sure Num Lock is turned off.

Understanding Dialog Boxes

A dialog box is displayed when a command requires more information.

When you choose a command name that is followed by an ellipsis (...), Microsoft Excel displays a dialog box so that you can provide more information. Depending on the dialog box, you type the information or select from a group of options.

For example, the Format Font dialog box is displayed when you choose the Format Font command. In the dialog box, you tell Microsoft Excel which font you want.

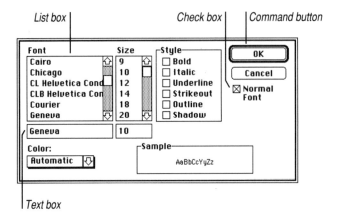

Every dialog box has one or more of the following areas to help you supply the information necessary to carry out the command.

Command button   You choose a command button to carry out the command, cancel the command, or display more options. Choose the OK button to complete a command or the Cancel button to cancel a command.

Command buttons use the same conventions as commands on menus. If a button is dimmed, it is unavailable. An ellipsis following the name of a command button means that more options are available. Choosing that command button expands the dialog box or displays another dialog box.

Text box   You type information in a text box. In the Formula Find dialog box, for example, you can type the information you want to find in the Find What box.

List box   Available choices are listed in a list box. In the File New dialog box, for example, you can select the type of document you want to create from the New box. If the list is longer than the box, you can use the scroll bar to see the rest of the list.

Option buttons   You can select only one option at a time from a group of option buttons. In the Format Alignment dialog box, for example, you can select the General, Left, Center, Right, or Fill option. A selected option button has a black dot in its center. To see what option buttons look like, see the illustration of the Edit Paste Special dialog box in the section, "Copying Cell Attributes Selectively," in Lesson 4.

Check boxes   You turn on check boxes to select options that are independent of one another, so you can select more than one at a time. For example, in the Options Workspace dialog box, you can turn on or turn off the R1C1, Status Bar, Tool Bar, Scroll Bars, Formula Bar, and Note Indicator check boxes to change your workspace. When a check box is turned on, an X appears inside the box.

Selecting Dialog Box Options

To move around in a dialog box, you can either click the item you want or press COMMAND and the key for the underlined letter at the same time.

Selecting options with the mouse   Use the procedures in this table to select options in a dialog box with the mouse.

To use the mouse to	Do this
Select an option	Click the option button.
Turn a check box on or off	Click the check box.
Select an item in a list box	Click the item.
Select text in a text box	Double-click a word, or drag through the characters.
Scroll through a list box	Use the scroll bars.

After you've selected the options you want, click the OK button to carry out the command. To cancel the command, click the Cancel button.

Selecting options with the keyboard   You can also select options in a dialog box with the keyboard. Choose the Options Workspace command and select the On option under Command Underlines. In a dialog box, press COMMAND+ the underlined letter for the option you want. Use the ARROW keys to scroll through lists.

Selecting command buttons with the keyboard   Press ENTER to choose the default button (the button with a dark border). Usually this is the OK button, which carries out the command. Press COMMAND+PERIOD or ESC to choose the Cancel button and cancel the command.

Creating a New Document

You can open and work with several documents at the same time.

When you create a new document in Microsoft Excel, it is displayed in its own window. You can have many document windows open at the same time.

The File New command You use the File New command to create a new document. You name the document when you save it.

Choose File New

Now you will create a new blank worksheet.

1 Point to File and drag to New.

✍ Press COMMAND+N.

Microsoft Excel displays the File New dialog box.

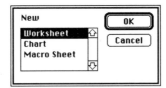

The File New dialog box lists the types of documents you can create: worksheet, chart, or macro sheet. "Worksheet" is already selected by default, so you can just choose the OK button.

2 Click the OK button.

✍ Press ENTER.

Microsoft Excel displays a new worksheet named Worksheet2. Worksheet1 is still open behind Worksheet2.

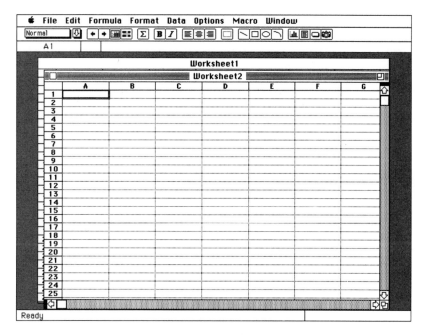

Switching Between Windows

The active document window contains the worksheet you're working on.

You can only work on the document in the active window. You can tell which document window is active by the dark title bar and dark border.

When you have more than one document open, you can switch to another document by choosing the document name from the bottom of the Window menu. All open windows are listed alphabetically and numbered at the bottom of the Window menu. The active window has a check mark next to its name.

You can also switch between windows by using the mouse to move and size windows until the one you want is visible, and then clicking anywhere in the window. With the keyboard, press COMMAND+M. If you have an extended keyboard, you can also press COMMAND+F6 to switch to the next window and COMMAND+SHIFT+F6 to switch to the previous window.

Switch to the Worksheet1 window

▶ Click any visible part of Worksheet1.

    ✒ Point to <u>W</u>indow and drag to <u>1</u> Worksheet1.

The Worksheet1 window is now active. When document windows overlap, the active window is in front.

Moving, Sizing, and Arranging Windows

The Window Arrange All command With Window Arrange All, you can quickly lay out all the open document windows so that none overlap. This way, you can see all open document windows at the same time. You can also use Window Arrange All to fit a single document window to the workspace. If you later display your document on a computer with a different size screen, such as a portable computer, your document will still fill the workspace exactly.

Arrange all windows on the workspace

▶ Point to Window and drag to Arrange All.

Both windows are arranged to fill the workspace. You can tell that Worksheet1 is the active window by the presence of scroll bars and the dark title bar.

Zoom box

	File Edit Formula Format Data Options Macro Window

Size box

Enlarging a window You can quickly enlarge a window to fill the entire workspace. Click the zoom box or drag the size box until the window fills the workspace.

Enlarge the Worksheet1 window

▶ In the upper-right corner of Worksheet1, click the zoom box.

The Worksheet1 window fills the the entire workspace.

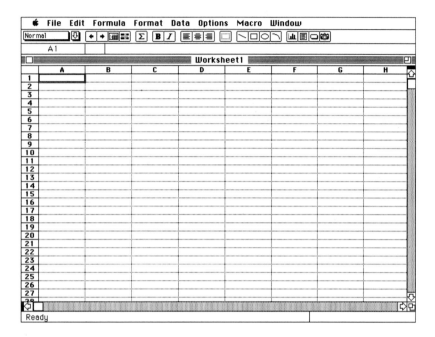

Restoring a window   You can quickly restore the window to its previous size. Click the zoom box with the mouse.

Restore the Worksheet1 window

▶ In the upper-right corner of the worksheet, click the zoom box.

The Worksheet1 window returns to its previous size.

Sizing a window manually   You can make a window the exact size you want by dragging the size box with the mouse. The size box is in the lower-right corner of the document window.

Size the Worksheet1 window

Make the Worksheet1 window shorter and wider.

▶ In the lower-right corner of the window, drag the size box up and right.

Your sized Worksheet1 window should look like this:

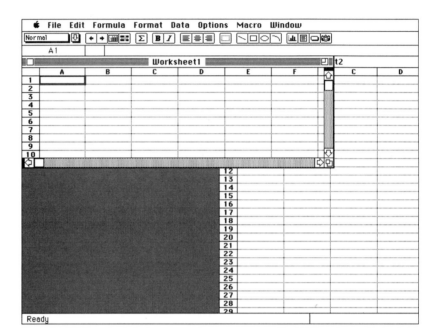

Moving a window   You can move a window anywhere you want within the workspace by dragging the title bar with the mouse.

Move the Worksheet1 window

Move the Worksheet1 window to the middle of the screen.

▶ Drag the Worksheet1 title bar down and right.

Your moved Worksheet1 window should look like this:

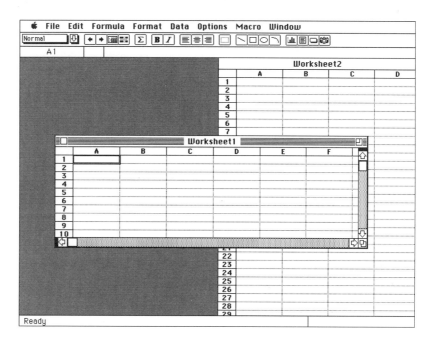

Getting Online Help

Microsoft Excel includes Help, a complete online reference tool, and an online HyperCard Tutorial. You can get information online in several ways.

To get information online	Do this
By category	Choose Window Help and use the Index.
While working on a task	Press COMMAND+SHIFT+? for context-sensitive Help.
To learn Microsoft Excel	Use the Microsoft Excel Tutorial. To start the Tutorial, go back to the Finder and double-click the Tutorial icon.

Display the list of Help topics

▶ Point to <u>W</u>indow and drag to <u>H</u>elp.

   ✍   Press COMMAND+SLASH (/).

The Help Index appears. You can click any underlined word to see that topic.

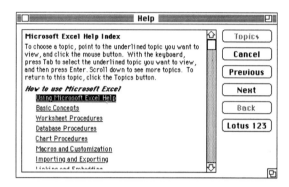

Get help on Help

The Using Microsoft Excel Help topic gives you information on how to use Help.

▶ Select the Using Microsoft Excel Help topic.

A list of topics and procedures for using Help appears in the Help window.

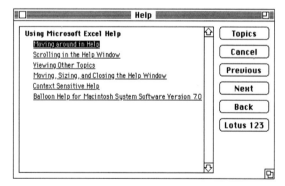

View other Help topics

1 Click the Topics button at the right of the Help window.

2 Click the down scroll arrow to scroll down to the Reference section.

3 Click the Commands topic.

4 Click the name of any menu.

A description of the commands on that menu appears in the window.

The Previous, Next, and Back buttons   With the Previous or Next button, you can move from your current topic to the previous or next topic in the sequence. With the Back button, you can move to the last topic you viewed.

Go back to the Help Index

Retrace your steps to the Help Index.

▶ Click the Back button twice.

The Help Index is redisplayed.

Use Help to look up Microsoft Excel equivalents of 1-2-3 commands.

Getting Help switching to Microsoft Excel   If you have worked with Lotus 1-2-3, you can use Help to look up the command equivalents for Microsoft Excel.

If you are familiar with Lotus 1-2-3, go through the next Help exercise to use your knowledge of 1-2-3 to learn about Microsoft Excel.

The Lotus 1-2-3 button   When you choose the Lotus 1-2-3 button, a dialog box is displayed. In the Command box, you can type the keystrokes of a specific 1-2-3 command for which you want to learn the Microsoft Excel equivalent. If you would rather see general Help on Microsoft Excel for 1-2-3 users, just choose OK in the dialog box.

Find the Microsoft Excel equivalent of File Retrieve (optional)

1 Choose the Lotus 1-2-3 button.

2 In the Command box, type **/fr**

3 Click OK.

   ✎ Press ENTER.

Help displays the procedure for choosing the File Open command.

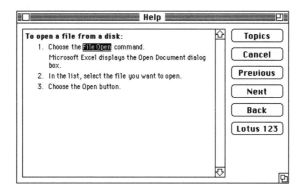

Quit Microsoft Excel Help

▶ Click the close box.

   ✎ Press COMMAND+W.

Closing Document Windows

You can choose the File Close command to close a window or you can click the close box with the mouse. If you have made any changes to the worksheet that you haven't saved, Microsoft Excel displays a dialog box asking if you want to save changes.

The File Close command   File Close closes the active document window.

Close the worksheet windows

Now you will close both worksheet windows.

1 Point to <u>F</u>ile and drag to <u>C</u>lose.

    ✑   Press COMMAND+W.

2 Click the close box to close the remaining worksheet.

Both document windows are closed. Microsoft Excel is still running with the null menu bar displayed.

Null menu bar

The null menu bar You see the null menu bar when all document windows are closed. The null menu bar contains only the File, Edit, and Window menus. Some of the commands that are usually on other menus move to the File menu when all document windows are closed.

Quitting Microsoft Excel

When you quit Microsoft Excel, it is no longer in memory.

The File Quit command File Quit ends a Microsoft Excel session. If you have any open document windows with unsaved changes, Microsoft Excel displays a dialog box for each of them, asking if you want to save changes.

Quit Microsoft Excel

▶ Point to <u>F</u>ile and drag to <u>Q</u>uit.

    ✑   Press COMMAND+Q.

Summary and Preview

In this lesson, you learned to:

Start and end a Microsoft Excel session   You started Microsoft Excel by double-clicking the Microsoft Excel icon and ended a session by choosing the File Quit command.

Work with windows   You moved and sized document windows.

Choose commands from menus   You chose commands from menus with the mouse or the keyboard.

Select options in dialog boxes   You learned about various types of dialog box options, including text boxes, list boxes, check boxes, and option buttons.

Create a new document   You created a document by using the File New command.

Get Help   You learned how to get Help while working with your document.

In the next lesson, you'll start creating a worksheet for a projected budget. You will open a worksheet, enter and edit data, and create formulas.

2 Designing and Documenting Your Worksheets

Creating a Worksheet

You will learn to:

- Move around in a worksheet and select cells.
- Open a document from a disk.
- Save and rename a document.
- Enter text, numbers, and formulas in cells.
- Edit and clear cell entries.
- Use references and functions in formulas.

Estimated lesson time: 45 minutes

In this lesson, you'll open a worksheet from the Practice folder and begin creating a monthly budget. You'll enter row and column titles to label items, and you'll enter some budget figures for July, the first month of the fiscal year. You'll finish by writing formulas using cell references and Microsoft Excel functions.

This lesson assumes that you know how to choose menu commands and select dialog box options, but you'll still get some hints.

For more information on	See in the *Microsoft Excel User's Guide*
Opening documents The parts of a worksheet Moving and selecting cells Entering data in a worksheet Editing characters in the formula bar Creating formulas	Chapter 3, "Creating and Using a Worksheet"
Clearing cell entries	Chapter 4, "Editing a Worksheet"

Start the lesson

If you quit Microsoft Excel at the end of Lesson 1, or are beginning the tutorial with this lesson, start Microsoft Excel now.

▶ Start Microsoft Excel.

Understanding the Worksheet

For an overview of Microsoft Excel worksheets, see the online Tutorial.

Run the Tutorial (optional)

1 Go back to the Finder. If you are running MultiFinder, click the icon in the upper-right corner of your screen. Otherwise, you will have to quit Microsoft Excel.

2 Double-click the Tutorial icon.

3 Click Worksheets.

4 Click Using a Worksheet.

5 Follow the instructions on the screen.

6 To quit the Tutorial, click the question mark in the lower-right corner; then click Quit.

Now that you know how to work with document windows in general, here are some important parts of the Microsoft Excel worksheet window:

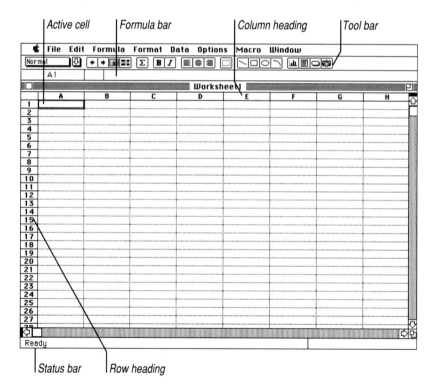

A Microsoft Excel worksheet has 256 columns, labeled A through IV, and 16,384 rows. The worksheet menu bar contains the commands you use with worksheets. The *tool bar* contains drawing tools, a style box, and buttons for formatting, alignment, and outlining. You will learn how to use these tools later in this book. You enter and edit cell data in the *formula bar*. The *status bar* displays messages from Microsoft Excel. The status bar now displays the message "Ready," meaning that Microsoft Excel is ready for you to choose a command or type data in a cell.

Moving Around the Worksheet

Cell A1 is the *active cell* when you first open a worksheet or macro sheet. Data you enter is stored in the active cell. You can identify the active cell by its dark border. When you select another cell, it becomes the active cell. You can select cells with the mouse or the keyboard.

Using the mouse to make another cell active   Click the cell you want to move to. If you can't see the cell you want in the window, use the scroll bars to scroll through the window and then click the cell.

Using the keyboard to make another cell active   The keys you can use to select cells in Microsoft Excel are listed in the following table. Some of these keys are available only on extended keyboards.

To move	Press
Left one cell	LEFT ARROW
Right one cell	RIGHT ARROW
Up one cell	UP ARROW
Down one cell	DOWN ARROW
Up one screen	PAGE UP
Down one screen	PAGE DOWN
To start of row	HOME
To end of row	END
To start of worksheet	COMMAND+HOME
To end of worksheet	COMMAND+END

Opening a Document from a Disk

Close the blank worksheet

Close the Worksheet1 window before you open the LESSON02 worksheet.

▶ Choose File Close.

    ✍ Press COMMAND+W.

The File Open command   With File Open, you open a document from a disk and display it in a window. You can open a Microsoft Excel worksheet, chart or macro sheet. You can also open a Lotus 1-2-3 worksheet with File Open.

Changing the current folder   You can also use File Open to change the current folder. Just click a folder name in the Open Document box and choose the Open button. To move to a higher folder, point to the folder name at the top of the list box and drag to select a folder. To change disk drives, choose the Drive button or the Desktop button if you're using Apple system software version 7.0.

Open the LESSON02 worksheet

1 Choose File Open.

    ✍ Press COMMAND+O.

2 In the Open Document box, double-click the Practice folder.

    ✍ Use the ARROW keys to select the Practice folder; then press ENTER.

3 Click LESSON02. Use the scroll bar in the list box to scroll to the filename.

    ✍ Use the ARROW keys to select LESSON02.

4 Choose the Open button.

	A	B	C	D	E
1	Title	WCS Cash Budget: 1992 Fiscal Year			

Arrange the LESSON02 window

You can use the Window Arrange All command to arrange a single window to fill the screen. You can also click the zoom box to enlarge the worksheet.

▶ Choose Window Arrange All.

Saving a Worksheet

In this lesson, you'll create a budget worksheet for a fictitious company, West Coast Sales. You can start now by renaming LESSON02 with the name you want.

The File Save As command   Use File Save As when you need to name a document that you're saving for the first time, or if you want to rename an existing document. You type the name in the dialog box that appears. You also use File Save As to save a document in a different file format.

The File Save command   After you've named your document with File Save As, you can choose File Save whenever you want to save your changes. The current version of your document replaces the previous version on the disk. If you choose File Save before you've named a document, Microsoft Excel displays the File Save As dialog box and prompts you for a name.

Save the worksheet as BUDGET

1   Choose File Save As.

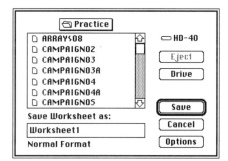

2   In the Save Worksheet As box, type **BUDGET**

You can also type a filename extension, such as .XLS, to help you identify the file as a worksheet.

3   Choose the Save button.

"BUDGET" now appears in the title bar of the active window.

Entering Text on a Worksheet

You'll start your projected budget worksheet for West Coast Sales (WCS) by entering text in column B to label the rows. You will label other worksheet areas with descriptions such as Introduction, Purpose, and so on. When you document your worksheets, you and others can understand their purpose, logic, and assumptions, and they'll be easier to use.

Microsoft Excel shows your entry in the active cell as you type.

As soon as you start typing, whatever you type appears in both the active cell and the formula bar. The *cancel box* and *enter box* appear in the formula bar, and the message in the status bar changes from "Ready" to "Enter."

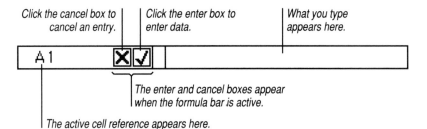

Click the cancel box to cancel an entry.

Click the enter box to enter data.

What you type appears here.

The enter and cancel boxes appear when the formula bar is active.

The active cell reference appears here.

Press ENTER to enter data or ESC to cancel a cell entry.

You can store your data in the active cell by clicking the enter box in the formula bar or by pressing ENTER. You can cancel the entry by clicking the cancel box in the formula bar or by pressing COMMAND+PERIOD or ESC.

If you make a mistake while you're typing, you can use the DELETE key or the OPTION+ARROW keys to move the *insertion point*, the blinking vertical line that shows where text is entered in the formula bar.

Enter the heading information

As you type the row titles, long entries will appear to spill into other columns, even though they are stored in column B. You'll learn to change column width in Lesson 3, "Formatting a Worksheet."

Remember, a step marked by a key icon (⌨) is a keyboard alternative to the preceding step.

1   Click cell A3.

⌨   Press the ARROW keys until cell A3 is selected.

2   Type **Created by**

3   Click the enter box.

⌨   Press ENTER.

4   Click cell B3.

⌨   Press the RIGHT ARROW key to select cell B3.

5   Type your name.

6   Click the enter box.

⌨   Press ENTER.

If you pressed RETURN instead of ENTER and the active cell changed, choose Options Workspace and turn off the Move Selection After Return check box.

You can use the ARROW keys to enter data and move to the next cell in one step.

Entering and moving in one step   You don't need to press ENTER after entering text in each cell. You can enter data and move to the next cell in a single step with either the mouse or the keyboard. With the mouse, type your entry and then click the next cell where you want to enter data. With the keyboard, type your entry and then press an ARROW key.

Enter row titles for the gross revenue items

1   Click cell A5.

⌨   Press the ARROW keys until cell A5 is selected.

2   Type **Fiscal Model Area**

3   Click cell B7.

⌨   Press the ARROW keys until cell B7 is selected.

4   Type **Gross Revenue**

5   Click the enter box.

⌨   Press ENTER.

Your worksheet should look like this:

	A	B	C	D	E
1	Title	WCS Cash Budget: 1992 Fiscal Year			
2					
3	Created by	Sam Bryan			
4					
5	Fiscal Model Area				
6					
7		Gross Revenue			
8					

You can save time entering data in a range of cells if you select all the cells in the range first. As you enter data in each cell, the next selected cell becomes the active cell in a top-to-bottom, left-to-right order.

To select a cell range	Do this
With the mouse	Drag from the first cell to the last cell in the range.
With the keyboard	Hold down SHIFT and press the ARROW keys to extend the selection.

Select a cell range and enter the row titles

Start by selecting cells B8 through B17, where you will enter the titles for Gross Revenue and Cost of Goods Sold. The first cell you select remains the active cell. After you select the cells, enter the data shown in the following illustration. If you make a typing mistake and want to move backwards through the selection, hold down the SHIFT key and click the enter box or press ENTER.

1 Drag from cell B8 to cell B17.

    ✍ Select cell B8; then press SHIFT+DOWN ARROW to extend the selection to cell B17.

2 Type the remaining entries, as shown in the following illustration.

3 After each entry, click the enter box.

    ✍ Press ENTER. Pressing an ARROW key removes the selection.

	A	B	C	D	E
1	Title	WCS Cash Budget: 1992 Fiscal Year			
2					
3	Created by	Sam Bryan			
4					
5	Fiscal Model Area				
6					
7		Gross Revenue			
8		Sales			
9		Shipping			
10		Total			
11					
12		Cost of Goods Sold			
13		Goods			
14		Freight			
15		Markdowns			
16		Miscellaneous			
17		Total			
18					

When you reach the last selected cell and click the enter box or press ENTER, the first selected cell becomes the active cell again.

Editing Cell Data

You can change a cell entry by typing a new entry over the old one. If you want to edit the existing entry without typing the new one from scratch, you can edit the entry in the formula bar. The formula bar displays the contents of the active cell.

Click the formula bar or press COMMAND+U to edit a cell.

You can activate the formula bar with either the mouse or keyboard. With the mouse, click anywhere in the formula bar. You can click the part of the entry you want to edit. To activate the formula bar with the keyboard, press COMMAND+U. Press COMMAND+PERIOD or ESC to return to the worksheet.

The movement and selection keys work differently in the formula bar than in the worksheet. In the formula bar, the ARROW keys move one character at a time, the HOME key moves the insertion point to the start of the entry, and the END key moves it to the end of the entry.

Select the text you want to edit; then choose the command.

With Microsoft Excel, you always select the data you want to act on before you choose the command. You can select the text you want to change with the mouse or keyboard.

To use the mouse to select	Do this
A word	Double-click the word.
Any character or sequence of characters	Drag across the character or sequence of characters.

To use the keyboard to select	Do this
Any character or group of characters	1 Press COMMAND+U to activate the formula bar.
	2 Press the LEFT ARROW key and position the insertion point at the start of the selection.
	3 Hold down SHIFT and press the ARROW keys to move to the end of the selection.

If you want to cancel your editing changes and restore the previous cell entry, click the cancel box or press COMMAND+PERIOD or ESC before entering the change.

Edit a cell entry

1 Click cell A5.

   ⌨ Press the ARROW keys until cell A5 is selected.

2 Click the formula bar.

   ⌨ Press COMMAND+U.

3 Select "Fiscal" by double-clicking it.

4 Type **Budget**

5 Click the enter box.

   ⌨ Press ENTER.

Entering Dates

With Microsoft Excel, you can enter a date or other number the way you want it formatted.

To enter dates in a Microsoft Excel worksheet, just type the date the way you want it to appear. Microsoft Excel formats the date the way you typed it and stores a serial number representing the date in the cell.

Microsoft Excel distinguishes between text and numbers. If you enter only numeric characters, your entry is a number. If you enter any alphabetic characters, it's text.

Enter a date

If you want to divide 7 by 1 by 91, type an equal sign (=) first to indicate you're entering a formula instead of a date.

Type a date in cell C6 to see how Microsoft Excel recognizes dates and formats them automatically. You can tell the date is a number because it's right-aligned.

1 Click cell C6.

    ✍ Press the ARROW keys until cell C6 is selected.

2 Type **7/1/91**

    This is the first day of Fiscal Year 1992.

3 Click the enter box.

    ✍ Press ENTER.

Clearing Cell Entries and Formats

The Edit Clear command   With Edit Clear, you can selectively clear cell attributes, such as formatting, or you can clear everything from the cell at once.

You can press DELETE and then ENTER to clear a cell entry.

The DELETE key   You can quickly clear a cell entry by pressing DELETE and then pressing ENTER.

Clear the format from the cell

Use the Edit Clear command to clear only the formatting from cell C6.

1 Choose Edit Clear.

2 Under Clear, select the Formats option.

3 Choose OK.

The serial number that represents the date, 31958, appears in the cell.

Type a date in a different format

Microsoft Excel can recognize a number format you type.

Now that the cell's format has been cleared, Microsoft Excel will format the cell according to a new date format you type.

1 In cell C6, type **Jul-91**

    This entry replaces the serial number.

2 Click the enter box.

    ✍ Press ENTER.

Entering Column Titles

You could type all the names of the months as column titles, but you can save time with the Data Series command.

The Data Series command   The Data Series command enters a sequence of numbers or dates in a range of cells.

Use context-sensitive Help to learn about the Data Series command

1 Press COMMAND+SHIFT+QUESTION MARK.

If you have an extended keyboard, you can also press SHIFT+F1 or SHIFT+HELP.

The mouse pointer turns into a question mark.

2 Choose Data Series.

3 Read the information about the Data Series command.

4 To close the Help window, click the close box.

You can also choose the command first and then press COMMAND+ SHIFT+QUESTION MARK while the dialog box is displayed.

You will be using Help throughout this book to learn more about Microsoft Excel features and commands.

Use the Data Series command to enter column titles

Remember to select cells before you choose a command in Microsoft Excel.

As with all Microsoft Excel commands, first select the cells you want to act on, and then choose the command you want.

You'll select 12 cells across the columns and then choose the Data Series command. When your selection reaches the edge of the window, the window begins to scroll.

1 Drag from cell C6 to cell N6.

✐ With cell C6 selected, press SHIFT+RIGHT ARROW to extend the selection to cell N6.

2 Choose Data Series.

Under Type, the Date option is already selected.

3 Under Date Unit, select the Month option.

4 Choose OK.

5 Click the scroll bar to scroll back to the active cell.

Your worksheet should look like this:

	A	B	C	D	E
1	Title	WCS Cash Budget: 1992 Fiscal Year			
2					
3	Created by	Sam Bryan			
4					
5	Budget Model Area				
6			Jul-91	Aug-91	Sep-91
7		Gross Revenue			
8		Sales			

Entering Data

Enter the budget figures for July

You'll save time by selecting the range of cells where you want to enter data and then clicking the enter box or pressing ENTER after each entry.

1 Drag from cell C8 to cell C16.

✎ Select cell C8 and then press SHIFT+DOWN ARROW to extend the selection to cell C16.

2 Enter the data for July, as shown in the following illustration.

	A	B	C	D	E
1	Title	WCS Cash Budget: 1992 Fiscal Year			
2					
3	Created by	Sam Bryan			
4					
5	Budget Model Area				
6			Jul-91	Aug-91	Sep-91
7		Gross Revenue			
8		Sales	26900		
9		Shipping	5550		
10		Total			
11					
12		Cost of Goods Sold			
13		Goods	17710		
14		Freight	270		
15		Markdowns	1240		
16		Miscellaneous	96		
17		Total			
18					

Entering Formulas

Begin a formula with an equal sign (=). You can also type + or – to begin a formula or @ to begin a function; Microsoft Excel converts any of these to an equal sign.

Use a colon (:) to indicate a cell range.

A formula can consist of numbers, arithmetic operators, cell references, and functions. You can create a formula by typing, by pointing to cells with the keyboard or the mouse, and by pasting names and functions.

To tell Microsoft Excel you're entering a formula in a cell, begin the entry with an equal sign (=).

References in formulas A reference in a formula can be the address of a cell or cell range. To indicate a range of cells, you use a colon (:) between the first and last cells; for example, B7:B9 refers to cells B7 through B9. To indicate a list of cells, you use a comma; for example, B7,D3,H9 refers to cell B7, cell D3, and cell H9.

Functions in formulas Microsoft Excel has 146 *worksheet functions* to help you perform specialized calculations easily. A worksheet function is a special built-in formula that performs an operation on the values you provide. For example, the formula =SUM(C22:C26) uses a function to add the values in the cell range C22:C26. It returns the same result as the formula =C22+C23+C24+C25+C26, which adds the values individually. Functions can be used alone or they can be nested within other functions. You can enter a function by typing it or by using the Formula Paste Function command.

Arguments in functions The arguments to a function tell Microsoft Excel how you want the function carried out. For example, when you use the SUM function, you need to specify which numbers or cells you want summed. The arguments appear in parentheses after the function name. Individual arguments are separated by commas.

You'll create all the formulas for your budget model in a single column. In Lesson 4, "Copying and Moving Cell Data and Formats," you'll copy the formulas to the other columns.

Type a formula

Create a formula in cell C10 to find the sum of the gross revenue items in cells C8 and C9. Remember that you begin a formula by typing an equal sign (=) and indicate a cell range by using a colon (:).

1 Click cell C10.

   ◈ Use the ARROW keys to move to cell C10.

Microsoft Excel makes sure you enter matching parentheses within formulas.

When you enter parentheses in a formula, Microsoft Excel momentarily displays matching parentheses in bold. Notice what happens in the formula bar as you type the first formula.

2 Type **=sum(c8:c9)**

3 Click the enter box.

   ◈ Press ENTER.

The total of Sales and Shipping, 32,450, appears in cell C10.

Formula Paste Function puts the function you want in your formula without typing.

The Formula Paste Function command   With Formula Paste Function, you can select the function you want from a list of all available worksheet functions. Formula Paste Function is especially useful when you create formulas by pointing with the mouse instead of by typing. If you begin a formula by pasting a function, Microsoft Excel adds the equal sign to the beginning of your formula automatically.

Pointing to add references to formulas   While the formula bar is active, you can use the mouse or the keyboard to point to cells whose references you want to use in the formula. The cells you point to are surrounded by a dotted line called the *marquee*.

Create a formula by pointing

Create a formula in cell C17 to sum the items under Cost of Goods Sold. You'll use the pointing method and the Formula Paste Function command to create the formula.

1 Click cell C17.

   ✐   Use the ARROW keys to move to cell C17.

2 Choose Formula Paste Function.

3 In the Paste Function box, scroll to SUM( ).

4 Click SUM( ) or use the DOWN ARROW key to select it.

5 Turn off the Paste Arguments check box.

6 Choose OK.

7 Drag from cell C13 to cell C16.

   ✐   Press the UP ARROW key to move the marquee to cell C13. Press SHIFT+DOWN ARROW to extend the marquee to cell C16.

8 Click the enter box.

   ✐   Press ENTER.

The total Cost of Goods Sold, 19,316, appears in cell C17.

Create another formula by pointing

Cell C19 will contain your gross profit. You'll enter a formula to calculate the difference between gross revenue and cost of goods sold. This formula will contain only arithmetic operators and references.

1 Click cell C19.

    ✎ Press the DOWN ARROW key to select cell C19.

2 Type an equal sign (=).

3 Click cell C10.

    ✎ Press the UP ARROW key to move the marquee to cell C10.

4 Type a minus sign (–).

5 Click cell C17.

    ✎ Press the UP ARROW key to move the marquee to cell C17.

6 Click the enter box.

    ✎ Press ENTER.

The difference between Gross Revenues and Cost of Goods Sold, 13,134, appears in cell C19.

The auto-sum button   You can click the auto-sum button on the tool bar to paste the SUM function and a proposed cell range into the active cell. With the keyboard, press COMMAND+SHIFT+T. Click the button again or press ENTER to accept the proposed range and cancel the marquee.

                                  Auto-sum button

Use the auto-sum button

1 Click cell C33.

2 Click the auto-sum button on the tool bar.

    Microsoft Excel places the SUM function and a proposed cell range in cell C33. The marquee encloses cells C22:C32.

3 Click the auto-sum button again or click the enter box to accept the proposed range and enter the formula in the cell.

    ✎ Press ENTER.

The total of Expenses, 11,085, appears in cell C33.

Enter the last formula

1 In cell C35, type =**c19–c33**

2 Click the enter box.

    ✐   Press ENTER.

The difference between Gross Profit and Total Expenses, 2,049, appears in cell C35.

Save and close your worksheet

It's a good idea to save your work regularly.

1 Choose File Save.

    ✐   Press COMMAND+S.

2 Choose File Close.

    ✐   Press COMMAND+W.

The File Save command replaces your old file with the new, edited one. If you want to save your worksheet with a different name, use File Save As again.

You Try It

The West Coast Sales Copier marketing department has been given a budget of $250,000 to promote the license for their newest copier technology. You'll create a worksheet that adds the expenses already incurred and calculates how much is left in the budget.

Include the creator of the worksheet (type your name), the title of the worksheet, "WCS Copier Marketing Budget," and today's date. Save the worksheet as CAMPAIGN.

The marketing department has incurred the following expenses to date:

Category	Amount
Advertising	100,000
Telemarketing	25,000
Direct Mail	50,000
Clerical Support	10,000
Consultants	15,000
General Administration	5,000

When you are finished, you can open the CAMPAIGN02 worksheet in the Practice folder for comparison with your worksheet. Close both documents when you are finished.

Summary and Preview

In this lesson, you learned to:

Move around in a worksheet and select cells You used the keyboard and mouse to move around the worksheet. You selected cells and cell ranges in different ways.

Open a document from a disk You used the File Open command to open a worksheet from a disk.

Save and rename a document You used the File Save As command to rename a worksheet.

Enter text, numbers, and formulas in cells You used the keyboard and the mouse to enter text, numbers, and formulas into cells.

Edit and clear cell entries You edited cell entries in the formula bar, and cleared cell entries by selecting a cell and typing new data or choosing the Edit Clear command.

Use references and functions in formulas You created formulas by pointing and typing. You used the Formula Paste Function command to paste a function into a formula. You also used the auto-sum button to paste the SUM function and a cell range into a formula in one step.

In the next lesson, you'll learn how to format a worksheet.

Formatting a Worksheet

You will learn to:

- Change column width and row height.
- Format numbers.
- Create your own number formats.
- Change the alignment of cell entries.
- Create, apply, and change cell styles with different fonts, number formats, and character alignments.
- Change the worksheet display.
- Add borders and shading to cells.

Estimated lesson time: 40 minutes

In this lesson, you'll use Microsoft Excel's formatting and display features to dramatically improve your worksheet's appearance.

This lesson assumes you know how to make a cell active and select a range of cells with the mouse or keyboard. You drag across a range of cells to select it with the mouse. With the keyboard, you hold down the SHIFT key and press the ARROW keys.

For more information on any of the formatting techniques described in this lesson, see Chapter 5, "Formatting a Worksheet," in the *Microsoft Excel User's Guide*.

Start the lesson

Follow these steps to open LESSON03 and rename it BUDGET.

1 Start Microsoft Excel.

2 Choose File Open.

3 Select LESSON03.

4 Choose the Open button.

5 Choose File Save As.

6 In the Save Worksheet As box, type **BUDGET**

7 Choose the Save button.

If you created a worksheet in the previous lesson, you will see a message asking whether you want to replace the existing BUDGET worksheet. Choose the Yes button.

Selecting Cells and Ranges

Remember, select the cells you want and then choose the command.

Selecting cells first   As you format the worksheet, you select the cells you want to act on first and then choose the command you want. Whether you want to format a single cell, an entire row or column, or the entire worksheet, you first make the selection and then choose a command.

If you want to make a "global" formatting change, start by selecting the entire worksheet.

You may want to change the formatting of entire rows or columns or of the entire worksheet.

If you need to save memory and disk space, format only the cells and cell ranges you need, rather than the entire worksheet.

Selecting entire rows, columns, or the worksheet   The following tables list the mouse and keyboard procedures for selecting entire rows, columns, and worksheets.

To use the mouse to select	Do this
One row or column	Click the row or column heading.
Multiple contiguous rows or columns	Drag across the column or row headings.
An entire worksheet	Click the blank box in the upper-left corner of the worksheet grid.

To use the keyboard to select	Do this
One or more rows	Select a cell or range of cells and then press SHIFT+SPACEBAR to select the entire row or rows.
One or more columns	Select a cell or range of cells and then press COMMAND+SPACEBAR to select the entire column or columns.
An entire worksheet	Press COMMAND+SHIFT+SPACEBAR.

Changing Column Width

The Format Column Width command   With Format Column Width, you can change the width of one or more columns with the Best Fit button or define a width from 0 to 255 characters. You need to select at least one cell in each column you want to change before you choose the command. When you open a new worksheet, the standard column width is 10 characters.

The Best Fit button widens columns just enough to display the longest string of text or numbers.

The Best Fit button   When you choose Format Column Width and choose the Best Fit button, Microsoft Excel widens the selected columns so that the longest string of numbers or text is fully displayed in its own column and does not spill over into other columns.

You can also choose the Best Fit option with the mouse by double-clicking the column boundary to the right of the row heading.

Changing column width with the mouse   You don't need to choose a command to change column width with the mouse. Point to the column boundary to the right of the column heading and then drag it to the width you want. The mouse pointer changes to **↔** when you point to the boundary. If you want to change the width of more than one column at the same time, select all the columns and then drag any of the selected column boundaries to increase or decrease the width of the columns.

Change column width for the entire worksheet

You can also make changes that affect your entire worksheet. You will change the width of all the columns in the worksheet to 12 characters. First, you'll select the entire worksheet.

1   In the upper-left corner of the worksheet grid, click the blank box.

  ✏ Press COMMAND+SHIFT+SPACEBAR.

  The entire worksheet is selected.

2   Choose Format Column Width.

3   In the Column Width box, type **12**

4   Choose OK.

5   Click any cell to cancel the selection of the entire worksheet.

  ✏ Press an ARROW key to move to a different cell.

Change column width for column B

You want all the row titles in column B to fit within the column. When you want to size a column to just the right width, choose the Best Fit button in the Format Column Width dialog box. You can also use the mouse to visually adjust the column width.

1   Select cells B7:B35.

2   Choose Format Column Width.

3   Choose the Best Fit button.

Changing Row Height

You can also change row height by choosing a command or by dragging the mouse.

When you open a new worksheet, the standard row height is set to accommodate the normal font for your worksheet. When you change the size of a font in a cell, Microsoft Excel adjusts row height automatically.

You can use Format Row Height to increase the row height and make your worksheet more readable.

The Format Row Height command   You can change the height of one or more rows with the Format Row Height command. Row height is measured in points instead of characters. One inch equals 72 points.

The Standard Height check box   You can turn on the Standard Height check box to set the correct row height for the largest font in the row. With the Geneva 10 font, standard row height is 13 points.

The Hide and Unhide buttons   You can choose the Hide and Unhide buttons to hide and unhide rows on the worksheet. You can also hide rows by setting the row height to zero.

Change row height for row 11

You want row 11 to act as a border. Make row 11 about half as high as the other rows.

1   Select a cell in row 11.

2   Choose Format Row Height.

3   In the Row Height box, type **6**

4   Choose OK.

Your worksheet should look like this:

	A	B	C	D
1	Title	WCS Cash Budget: 1992 Fiscal Year		
2				
3	Created by	Sam Bryan		
4				
5	Budget Model Area			
6			Jul-91	Aug-91
7		Gross Revenue		
8		Sales	26900	
9		Shipping	5550	
10		Total	32450	
12		Cost of Goods Sold		
13		Goods	17710	
14		Freight	270	
15		Markdowns	1240	
16		Miscellaneous	96	
17		Total	19316	
18				
19		Gross Profit	13134	

Repeating a Format

With Edit Repeat, you can repeat a formatting change.

The Edit Repeat command   With the Edit Repeat command, you can repeat your most recent action. The name of the Edit Repeat command changes to reflect your last action; for example, Edit Repeat Column Width or Edit Repeat Row Height. To use the Edit Repeat command, you must use a menu command to perform the original action.

Repeat the row height for row 18

You want to set rows 18, 20, and 34 to the same row height as row 11. Since you just changed row height for row 11, you'll see Repeat Row Height in the Edit menu.

1   Select a cell in row 18.

2   Choose Edit Repeat Row Height.

    ✍   Press COMMAND+Y.

Selecting Multiple Cells and Cell Ranges

You can select and format multiple ranges at once.

How to make a multiple selection You can select multiple ranges at once. With the mouse, make your first selection and then hold down the COMMAND key while you make additional selections.

If you have a Macintosh extended keyboard, you can make multiple selections with the keyboard. Select the first range (by holding down SHIFT and pressing the ARROW keys), press SHIFT+F8 to turn on Add mode, move to the start of the next range you want to select, and press F8 to begin selecting that range. Repeat the sequence as needed.

Repeat the row height for rows 20 and 34 in one step

You can save time by selecting a cell in each of these rows and then choosing the Edit Repeat Row Height command only once.

1 Select a cell in row 20.

2 Hold down COMMAND and click a cell in row 34.

 ✐ Press SHIFT+F8 to keep the selected cell in row 20. Move to a cell in row 34. Press F8 to select the second cell.

3 Choose Edit Repeat Row Height.

 ✐ Press COMMAND+Y.

Formatting Numbers

The Format Number command With Format Number, you can format data with a built-in Microsoft Excel number format or your own custom number format. When you choose Format Number, you can select a format from the list or type your own format in the Format box.

You can create custom number formats with Microsoft Excel.

Custom number formats You use specific symbols to create custom number formats in Microsoft Excel. For example, to format a number this way:

4:06 am, on November 10, 1990

starting with this date entry and General format:

11/10/90 4:06

create this number format:

h:mm am/pm", on "mmmm d", "yyyy

Format a cell range for dollars

Format the Budget Area to display dollar values in whole numbers, with dollar signs, commas separating thousands, and negative numbers in parentheses. Start by selecting the cell range.

1 Select cells C7:N35.

2 Choose Format Number.

3 In the Format Number dialog box, select the first dollar format:
   $#,##0_);($#,##0).

4 Choose OK.

5 Scroll back to the active cell.

    ✍ Press COMMAND+DELETE.

Create a custom number format for the month titles

Now create a custom number format for the month titles. Instead of displaying the abbreviated name of the month and the year, display the full name of the month by typing "mmmm" in the Format box.

1 Select cells C6:N6.

2 Choose Format Number.

3 In the Format box at the bottom of the dialog box, type **mmmm**

   The selected text is replaced by what you type.

4 Choose OK.

5 Scroll back to the active cell.

    ✍ Press COMMAND+DELETE.

Your worksheet should look like this:

	A	B	C	D
1	Title	WCS Cash Budget: 1992 Fiscal Year		
2				
3	Created by	Sam Bryan		
4				
5	Budget Model Area			
6			July	August
7		Gross Revenue		
8		Sales	$26,900	
9		Shipping	$5,550	
10		Total	$32,450	
12		Cost of Goods Sold		
13		Goods	$17,710	
14		Freight	$270	
15		Markdowns	$1,240	
16		Miscellaneous	$96	
17		Total	$19,316	
19		Gross Profit	$13,134	
21		Expenses		

Aligning Cell Entries

By default, Microsoft Excel aligns text to the left and numbers to the right. You can change the alignment of text, numbers, and dates with the alignment buttons on the tool bar and the Format Alignment command.

You can change alignment in a cell by clicking the alignment buttons on the tool bar.

The alignment buttons   With the alignment buttons on the tool bar, you can quickly change the alignment of numbers or text within a cell or cell range. Select the cell or cell range and then click the left, center, or right alignment button.

Left alignment button | | Right alignment button

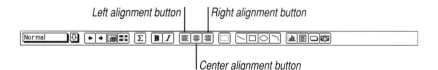

| Center alignment button

The Format Alignment command   With Format Alignment, you can change the alignment of text or numbers in the selected cells. The Left, Center, and Right options work just like the buttons on the tool bar. The General option, the default, aligns text to the left and numbers to the right. The Fill option repeats the characters in a cell to fill the entire cell. If you turn on the Wrap Text check box, text is wrapped within the cell so that all the text can be displayed in a narrower column width.

Center the month titles

Your month titles are numbers with a custom date format, so they're right-aligned. Since these serve as headings, you might want to change their alignment.

▶ With cells C6:N6 still selected, click the center alignment button on the tool bar.

Because of the "select-and-do" approach, you selected the month titles only once and then formatted them with two commands.

Right-align text in the worksheet area labels

1 Select cells A1:A5.

2 Choose Format Alignment.

3 Under Alignment, select the Right option.

4 Choose OK.

   You can also right-align the text by clicking the right alignment button on the tool bar, instead of doing steps 2 through 4.

5 Choose Format Column Width.

6 Choose the Best Fit button.

   You can also choose the Best Fit option by double-clicking the column A heading boundary instead of doing steps 5 and 6.

Your worksheet should look like this:

	A	B	C	D
1	Title	WCS Cash Budget: 1992 Fiscal Year		
2				
3	Created by	Sam Bryan		
4				
5	Budget Model Area			
6			July	August
7		Gross Revenue		
8		Sales	$26,900	
9		Shipping	$5,550	
10		Total	$32,450	
12		Cost of Goods Sold		
13		Goods	$17,710	
14		Freight	$270	
15		Markdowns	$1,240	
16		Miscellaneous	$96	
17		Total	$19,316	
19		Gross Profit	$13,134	

Changing Fonts

You can change text fonts to make your worksheet easier to read.

Font refers to the design of the characters in which text and numbers are displayed on the screen and printed by a printer. Each font has a name (such as Geneva, Helvetica, or Times), and comes in various sizes (such as 9 point or 12 point) and styles (such as normal, bold, or italic).

The screen fonts available in Microsoft Excel depend on your system configuration. The printer fonts available depend on the specific printers you've set up to work with Microsoft Excel.

The default screen font for Microsoft Excel is Geneva 10. The row and column headings appear in this font, and standard row height is set to accommodate Geneva 10. You can use an unlimited number of fonts with Microsoft Excel.

Row height adjusts for larger fonts. This feature is useful for presentations.

The Format Font command   You use the Format Font command to change the font for a cell or range of cells. You can use an unlimited number of fonts, styles, and sizes on your worksheet to help organize your data and create striking presentations. If you have a color monitor, you can use 16 colors on a worksheet to increase the range of visual effects available.

The normal font   Text and numbers appear formatted with the normal, or default, font until another font is applied. You use the Format Style command to change the normal font for your worksheet.

Change the worksheet title font

Now you'll change the font of the title from Geneva 10 point to Times 12 point and add bold formatting.

1 Select cells A1:B1.

2 Choose Format Font.

3 In the Font box, select Times.

4 Under Size, select 14.

5 Under Style, turn on the Bold check box.

6 Choose OK.

Your worksheet should look like this:

	A	B	C	D
1	Title	WCS Cash Budget: 1992 Fiscal Year		
2				
3	Created by	Sam Bryan		
4				
5	Budget Model Area			
6			July	August
7		Gross Revenue		
8		Sales	$26,900	
9		Shipping	$5,550	
10		Total	$32,450	
12		Cost of Goods Sold		
13		Goods	$17,710	
14		Freight	$270	
15		Markdowns	$1,240	
16		Miscellaneous	$96	
17		Total	$19,316	
19		Gross Profit	$13,134	

Using Cell Styles

Cell styles are an easy way to quickly and consistently apply cell attributes such as number formats, fonts, alignment, patterns, and protection.

The easiest way to create a style is by example. You format a cell or range with the attributes you want included in the style, and define that group of attributes as a style. You can then apply the style to other cells with similar types of data.

For example, you may want all summary totals bold, centered, and formatted as dollars. You apply this formatting to one cell and then define a style called Total for the formatting used in the cell. Instead of applying each format individually to the next cell, you just apply the Total style and the selected cell is instantly formatted. If you decide to change the style from bold to italic, all cells with the Total style change.

You can define a style by using the style box on the tool bar or the Format Style command.

The style box   You can use the style box to define a new style and to apply a style to other cells. First, format a cell using the Format Number, Format Alignment, Format Font, and Format Cell Protection commands. Click the style box, type a new style name, and press ENTER.

Style box

The Format Style command   You can also use the Format Style command to define and apply cell styles. First choose Format Style and type a name in the Style Name box. The Description box describes the style of the current selection. You can choose the Number, Font, Alignment, Pattern, and Protection buttons to open the respective dialog boxes and make any changes to the cell style. Choose the OK button to define the style.

Create a worksheet title cell style

Create a cell style based on the formatted worksheet title. Earlier in this lesson, you formatted the worksheet title in Times 12-point bold. You will name this style and then use it to format the other worksheet titles in cells A3 and A5.

1   Cells A1:B1 should still be selected.

2   Click the style box on the tool bar to select Normal.

3   Type **Title**

4   Press ENTER.

The Normal style hasn't been changed; instead, a new style has been created.

The worksheet title and area labels are aligned differently. Alignment is not part of the Title style.

Apply the Title cell style

1   Select cells A3 and A5.

2   In the style box on the tool bar, click the arrow to display the list.

3   Select the Title cell style.

Cells A1:B1, A3, and A5 are all formatted the same way.

	A	B	C	D
1	Title	**WCS Cash Budget: 1992 Fiscal Year**		
2				
3	**Created by**	Sam Bryan		
4				
5	**dget Model Area**			
6			July	August
7		Gross Revenue		
8		Sales	$26,900	
9		Shipping	$5,550	

Wrap the text to fit

The bold text is wider; it is now cut off by the left boundary of column A. You can wrap the text to fit within the column width.

1 With cells A3 and A5 still selected, choose Format Alignment.

2 Turn on the Wrap Text check box.

3 Choose OK.

Your worksheet should look like this:

	A	B	C	D
1	Title	WCS Cash Budget: 1992 Fiscal Year		
2				
3	Created by	Sam Bryan		
4				
5	Budget Model Area			
6			July	August
7		Gross Revenue		
8		Sales	$26,900	
9		Shipping	$5,550	
10		Total	$32,450	
12		Cost of Goods Sold		
13		Goods	$17,710	
14		Freight	$270	
15		Markdowns	$1,240	
16		Miscellaneous	$96	
17		Total	$19,316	
19		Gross Profit	$13,134	

Change the font of the Normal style

The Normal style includes the Geneva font. You can increase the speed of laser printing your worksheet by using fonts that reside on your printer. Use the Format Style command to change the Normal style font from Geneva to Helvetica.

1 Select cell C7.

2 Choose Format Style.

> ☑ To get Help on the Format Style command, press COMMAND+SHIFT+ QUESTION MARK while the Format Style dialog box is displayed.

3 In the Style Name box, select Normal.

4 Choose the Define button.

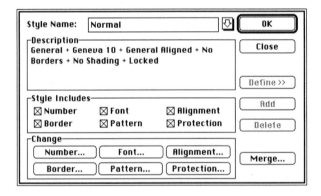

5 Under Change, choose the Font button.

6 In the Font box, select Helvetica.

7 Choose OK to select the Helvetica font.

8 Choose OK to define the style.

Create a heading style for row and column titles

To make the month titles stand out, use the bold button on the tool bar to make them bold.

1   Select cells C6:N6.

2   On the tool bar, click the bold button.

Bold button

3   Choose Format Style.

4   In the Style Name box, type **Heading**

5   Choose the Define button.

6   Under Style Includes, turn off the check boxes for Number, Border, Patterns, Alignment, and Protection, leaving only the Font check box turned on.

7   Choose OK to define the style.

Because you left only the Font attribute turned on, you can apply the Heading style to cells that are formatted for numbers and dates as well as text. Only the font will be changed.

Apply the Heading cell style

Apply the Heading style to the major category titles to make them stand out.

1   Scroll back to the active cell.

   ✐   Press COMMAND+DELETE.

2   Select cells B7, B12, B19, B21, and B35.

   Remember to use the COMMAND key to make a multiple selection.

3   In the style box on the tool bar, click the arrow to display the list of styles.

4   Select Heading.

Create a new style called Total

Now, you will define a new cell style with Helvetica 10-point bold italic. After you define the style in one cell, you will apply the style to other cells.

1 Select cell B10.

2 Choose Format Font.

3 Under Style, turn on the Bold and Italic check boxes.

4 Choose OK.

5 Click the style box on the tool bar to select Normal.

6 Type **Total**

7 Press ENTER to name the style.

8 Keeping cell B10 selected, select cells B17 and B33.

9 In the style list on the tool bar, select Total.

Changing a cell style   You can create a new cell style by changing an existing cell style. Remember to turn off the check boxes for any attributes you don't want included in the new style.

Format summary figures with bold and color

Format the Summary figures in column C with the Heading style, Helvetica 10-point bold. You will create another cell style that includes color by changing an existing style.

1 Select cells C10, C17, C19, C33, and C35.

2 Choose Format Style.

3 Choose the Define button.

4 In the Style Name list, select Heading.

5 Under Change, choose the Font button.

6   In the Color box, click the arrow to display the list.

If you do not have a color monitor, the names of the colors appear in the Color box instead of the colors themselves. If you later display the worksheet on a color monitor, the color formatting will appear.

7   In the Color list, select blue.

8   Choose OK to close the Format Font dialog box.

9   In the Style Name box, type **SumData**

10   Choose OK to close the Format Style dialog box.

11   Click another cell or press an ARROW key so you can see the color.

If you have a color monitor, the summary data in the selected cells appears in blue.

When you copy the budget figures to columns D through N in Lesson 4, you'll also copy the formats.

Changing the Worksheet Display

You can turn off gridlines to make a Microsoft Excel worksheet look like a prepared report.

The Options Display command   You can change the way your worksheet is displayed with the Options Display command. You can turn on or off the display of gridlines, row and column headings, zero values, outline symbols, and automatic page breaks. You can display formulas instead of values, and you can change the color of gridlines and row and column headings. These changes apply only to the active worksheet.

Turn off gridlines

1   Choose Options Display.

2   Under Cells, turn off the Gridlines check box.

3   Choose OK.

Adding Borders and Shading

You can use borders and shading to create presentation-quality worksheets and more usable templates. By using borders and shading, and by adjusting column width and row height, you can create visual effects such as a double-line border.

You can create seven types of solid vertical and horizontal borders with different shading patterns.

The Format Border command   With Format Border, you can add seven types of borders to a cell or range and vary the shading pattern in selected cells. You can outline a range of cells, or add borders to the top, bottom, left, or right sides of cells. You can also shade a range of cells. You can select from 18 shading patterns with the Format Patterns command.

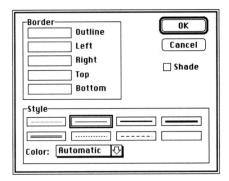

Create a border around each month title

Now you will create a border around each of the month titles.

1 Select cells C6:N6.

2 Choose Format Border.

3 Select the Outline option.

4 Select the Left option.

5 Under Style, select the third line style from the left.

6 Choose OK.

7 Select a cell outside your selection to see the outline border clearly.

Your worksheet should look like this:

	A	B	C	D	E
1	Title	WCS Cash Budget: 1992 Fiscal Year			
2					
3	Created by	Sam Bryan			
4					
5	Budget Model Area				
6			July	August	September
7		Gross Revenue			
8		Sales	$26,900		
9		Shipping	$5,550		
10		Total	$32,450		
12		Cost of Goods Sold			
13		Goods	$17,710		
14		Freight	$270		
15		Markdowns	$1,240		
16		Miscellaneous	$96		
17		Total	$19,316		
19		Gross Profit	$13,134		
21		Expenses			
22		Advertising	$4,000		

Outline the income and expense category titles

1 Select cells B7:B35.

2 Choose Format Border.

3 Select the Outline option.

4 Choose OK.

Format a cell with shading

Now you will shade and outline each of the narrow rows that divide major budget categories.

1 Select cell B11.

2 Choose Format Border.

3 Select the Outline option.

4 Turn on the Shade check box.

5 Choose OK.

Define a shaded border style to divide major budget categories

1 Choose Format Style.

2 In the Style Name box, type **Shade**

3 Choose the Define button.

4 Under Change, choose the Pattern button.

5 In the Pattern list, select the third pattern from the top.

6 Choose OK to close the Patterns dialog box.

7 Under Style Includes, turn off the Number, Font, Alignment, and Protection check boxes, leaving only the Border and Patterns check boxes turned on.

8 Choose OK to define the style.

The Formula Goto command   With Formula Goto, you can quickly "go to" (select) another cell. You can choose this command with either the mouse or the keyboard.

Apply the style

1 Choose Formula Goto.

   Press COMMAND+G.

2 In the Reference box, type **b18,b20,b34**

3 Choose OK.

   This selects cells B18, B20, and B34.

4 In the style list on the tool bar, select Shade.

Your worksheet should look like this:

	A	B	C	D	E
1	Title WCS Cash Budget: 1992 Fiscal Year				
2					
3	Created by Sam Bryan				
4					
5	Budget Model Area				
6			July	August	September
7		Gross Revenue			
8		Sales	$26,900		
9		Shipping	$5,550		
10		Total	$32,450		
12		Cost of Goods Sold			
13		Goods	$17,710		
14		Freight	$270		
15		Markdowns	$1,240		
16		Miscellaneous	$96		
17		Total	$19,316		
19		Gross Profit	$13,134		
21		Expenses			
22		Advertising	$4,000		
23		Salaries	$4,700		

Save and close your worksheet

Save your work before taking a break or continuing with the next lesson.

1 Choose File Save.

2 Choose File Close.

You Try It

In Lesson 2, you created a worksheet that calculated the budget for an ad campaign. In this lesson you will format that worksheet. If you did not go through the "You Try It" exercise in Lesson 2, you can use the worksheet provided.

Use the Microsoft Excel formatting commands to change the appearance of the worksheet. Format the title and create a Title style. Create a Heading style for the row and column labels and align all row labels to the right.

The sample file, suggested procedures, and resulting file provide suggestions for formatting the worksheet.

1 Open the CAMPAIGN03 worksheet.

2 Save it as CAMPAIGN.

3 Change the font, size, and style of the title.

4 Create a Title style.

5 Create a Heading style and apply it to the row labels.

6 Align the row labels to the right.

7 Turn off the worksheet gridlines.

8 Create an outline border around the row titles.

9 Decrease the row height between titles and listed expenses.

10 Shade the cells between the titles and listed expenses.

11 Format the numbers as dollars.

12 Open CAMPAIGN03A and compare it to your work.

You can use the Window Arrange All command to compare the worksheets.

13 Save the CAMPAIGN worksheet and close both worksheets when you are finished.

Summary and Preview

In this lesson, you learned to:

Change column width and row height You changed the column width and row height with the mouse by dragging the row or column boundary. You also used the Format Column Width and Format Row Height commands to change the row height and column width. You used the Best Fit button in the Format Column Width dialog box to adjust the column to accommodate all cell entries.

Format numbers You used the Format Number command to change number and date formats.

Create your own number formats You created a custom number format by editing a number format in the Format Number dialog box.

Change the alignment of cell entries You aligned cell entries with the alignment buttons on the tool bar and with the Format Alignment command.

Create, apply, and change cell styles You created and applied cell styles with the style box on the tool bar and with the Format Style command. You also created a new cell style by changing an existing style.

Change the worksheet display You used the Options Display command to turn off the display of gridlines.

Add borders and shading to cells You used the Format Border command to create borders within your worksheet.

In the next lesson, you will copy and move cell data and insert and delete rows, columns, and ranges. You'll also find out how to selectively copy cell entries or formats.

Copying and Moving Cell Data and Formats

You will learn to:

- Copy data to adjacent cells.
- Insert and delete rows, columns, and cells.
- Move cell data.
- Undo a command.
- Copy data to nonadjacent cells.
- Copy cell attributes selectively.

Estimated lesson time: 40 minutes

In this lesson, you'll insert and delete rows, columns, and cells. You'll also copy and move cell data and formats.

Many Microsoft Excel commands have keyboard shortcuts that bypass the menus entirely. In this lesson, keyboard shortcuts are listed in the procedural steps. You can choose commands by whichever method you find most convenient.

For more information on	See in the *Microsoft Excel User's Guide*
Creating formulas Using absolute and relative references	Chapter 3, "Creating and Using a Worksheet"
Moving and copying	Chapter 4, "Editing a Worksheet"

Start the lesson

Follow these steps to open LESSON04 and rename it BUDGET.

1 Open LESSON04.

2 Choose File Save As.

3 In the Save Worksheet As box, type **BUDGET**

4 Choose the Save button.

5 If you get a message asking if you want to replace the existing BUDGET worksheet, choose the Yes button.

Filling Adjacent Cells

To copy into adjacent cells you use the Edit Fill commands. The Edit Fill commands copy formulas, formats, or values from a range in a single row or column into an adjacent range with any number of rows or columns. You can copy in any direction.

Microsoft Excel offers time-saving Edit Fill commands for copying to adjacent cells.

The Edit Fill Right and Edit Fill Left commands   With Edit Fill Right, you can copy everything in the left column of a selection to the other columns in the selection. For example, you can choose Edit Fill Right to copy a fixed expense such as rent from the first month to the rest of the months. If you hold down SHIFT when you select the Edit menu, the command Fill Left appears in place of Fill Right. With Edit Fill Left, you can copy the right column of a selection to the other columns in the selection.

The Edit Fill Down and Edit Fill Up commands   With Edit Fill Down, you can copy everything in the top row of a selection to the other rows in the selection. For example, you can copy formulas that sum a budget expense for the year from the first expense item to each of the other expense items by choosing the Edit Fill Down command. The formulas adjust to calculate each expense correctly. If you hold down SHIFT when you select the Edit menu, the command Fill Up appears in place of Fill Down. With Edit Fill Up, you can copy the bottom row of a selection to the other rows in the selection.

Microsoft Excel offers keyboard shortcuts for bypassing menus.

Keyboard shortcuts   By using keyboard shortcuts, you can quickly carry out a command without displaying the menu. For example, you can press COMMAND+R instead of choosing the Edit Fill Right command and COMMAND+D instead of choosing the Edit Fill Down command. Microsoft Excel has many other useful keyboard shortcuts. Some keyboard shortcuts are listed in the menus next to the command names. The following table lists some additional keyboard shortcuts you can use in this lesson to copy and move data.

Command or action	Keyboard shortcut
Edit Copy	COMMAND+C
Edit Cut	COMMAND+X
Edit Delete	COMMAND+K
Edit Fill Down	COMMAND+D
Edit Fill Right	COMMAND+R
Edit Insert	COMMAND+I
Edit Paste	COMMAND+V
Select a column	COMMAND+SPACEBAR
Select a row	SHIFT+SPACEBAR

Many of the budget figures in your worksheet, such as Rent, are the same for each month. You'll copy the formulas for total revenues, cost of goods sold, gross profit, expenses, and operating income from July to the other 11 months.

Copy the figures from July to the other months

You'll use the Edit Fill Right command. First, you need to select a range including the cells in column C that you want to copy and the cells in all the other columns that you want to copy into.

1 Select cells C7:N35.

2 Choose Edit Fill Right.

   ✒ Press COMMAND+R.

3 Scroll back to the active cell.

   ✒ Press COMMAND+DELETE.

Your worksheet should look like this:

	A	B	C	D	E
1	Title	WCS Cash Budget: 1992 Fiscal Year			
2					
3	Created by	Sam Bryan			
4					
5	Budget Model Area				
6			July	August	September
7		Gross Revenue			
8		Sales	$26,900	$26,900	$26,900
9		Shipping	$5,550	$5,550	$5,550
10		Total	$32,450	$32,450	$32,450
12		Cost of Goods Sold			
13		Goods	$17,710	$17,710	$17,710
14		Freight	$270	$270	$270
15		Markdowns	$1,240	$1,240	$1,240
16		Miscellaneous	$96	$96	$96
17		Total	$19,316	$19,316	$19,316
19		Gross Profit	$13,134	$13,134	$13,134
21		Expenses			
22		Advertising	$4,000	$4,000	$4,000

You can copy both cell data and formats.

The formatting was also copied.

The formulas you copied from July adjust to the data for every other month. The cell ranges in each of the copied formulas reflect the column the formula is in.

The references in these formulas are relative references. When you copy a formula containing relative references, the references are adjusted to reflect the new location. However, absolute references always refer to the same cell regardless of where the formula is copied.

Relative references A relative reference describes the location of a cell in terms of its distance in rows and columns from another cell. Relative references are analogous to giving directions such as "Deliver newspapers to every third house." In the following worksheet, the formula in cell D17 sums the values in cells D13:D16. The formula in cell E17 sums the values in cells E13:E16. Likewise the formulas in F17 and G17 sum the values in cells F13:F16 and G13:G16 respectively.

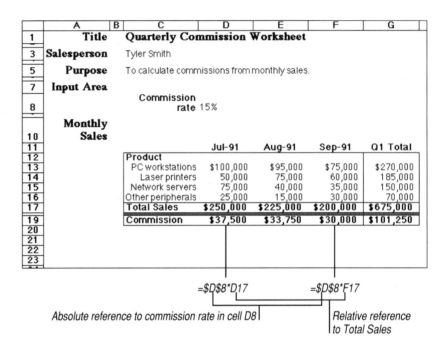

Absolute reference to commission rate in cell D8

Relative reference to Total Sales

Absolute references An absolute cell reference describes a specific cell address. Absolute references are analogous to giving directions such as "Deliver the newspaper to 403 Oak Street." In the previous illustration, the formulas in cells D19:F19 calculate commissions based on the total sales for each month. However, each of these formulas refers to cell $D$8, the cell that contains the commission rate (15 percent). The dollar signs ($) indicate an absolute reference to cell $D$8. No matter where the commission formula is copied, it always refers to cell $D$8.

Inserting Rows, Columns, and Cells

You use the same command to insert a cell, a row, or a column. The area you select before you choose the command determines what is inserted.

The Edit Insert command   With Edit Insert, you can insert a cell or range of cells into the worksheet. Edit Insert always inserts a cell range equal in size and shape to the selected cell range. The keyboard shortcut is COMMAND+I.

You can insert a cell, range of cells, column, or row with Edit Insert.

Inserting rows, columns, and cells   To insert a row, select the entire row below where you want to insert the new row, and then choose Edit Insert. To insert a column, select the entire column to the left of where you want to insert the new column, and then choose Edit Insert. You can insert multiple rows or columns by first selecting multiple rows or columns. If you want to insert a range of cells, select the range where you want the insertion and then choose Edit Insert. A dialog box appears, asking whether you want to shift the selected cells down or right.

Insert a column at column B

You'll need an extra column for some changes you'll make to the row titles. Insert a column at column B.

1   Select column B.

Remember, you can select a column by clicking the column heading or by selecting a cell in that column and pressing COMMAND+SPACEBAR.

2   Choose Edit Insert.

✐   You can also press COMMAND+I.

A new column is inserted at column B, shifting other columns to the right.

Your worksheet should look like this:

	A	B	C	D	E
1	**Title**		**WCS Cash Budget: 1992 Fiscal Year**		
2					
3	**Created by**		Sam Bryan		
4					
5	**Budget Model Area**				
6				July	August
7			Gross Revenue		
8			Sales	$26,900	$26,900
9			Shipping	$5,550	$5,550
10			*Total*	$32,450	$32,450
12			Cost of Goods Sold		
13			Goods	$17,710	$17,710
14			Freight	$270	$270
15			Markdowns	$1,240	$1,240
16			Miscellaneous	$96	$96
17			*Total*	$19,316	$19,316
19			Gross Profit	$13,134	$13,134
21			Expenses		
22			Advertising	$4,000	$4,000
23			Salaries	$4,700	$4,700

Deleting Rows, Columns, and Cells

You can delete a column or row with Edit Delete.

You use the Edit Delete command to delete a cell, a row, or a column. As with the Edit Insert command, the area you select before you choose the command determines what is deleted.

Deleting cells is different from clearing cells. The Edit Clear command clears the data within a cell, but does not delete the cell and move other cells.

You can also delete a range of cells with Edit Delete.

The Edit Delete command   With Edit Delete, you can delete a cell or range of cells from the worksheet and shift other cells to close the space. Edit Delete always deletes a cell range equal in size and shape to the selected cell range. The keyboard shortcut is COMMAND+K.

Deleting rows, columns, and cells   To delete a row, select the entire row and then choose Edit Delete. To delete a column, select the entire column and then choose Edit Delete. You can delete multiple rows or columns by first selecting multiple rows or columns. If you want to delete a range of cells, select the range and then choose Edit Delete. A dialog box appears, asking whether you want to shift cells up or left to fill the space.

Remember that the Edit Insert and Edit Delete commands physically move cells. If you insert or delete a partial row or column, cells could become separated from their supporting or dependent data.

Delete row 2

You want to move the figures closer to the worksheet title. Delete row 2 to move the rest of the worksheet up one row.

1   Select row 2.

Remember, you can select a row by clicking the row heading or by selecting a cell in that row and pressing SHIFT+SPACEBAR.

2   Choose Edit Delete.

✍   Press COMMAND+K.

All cells below row 2 shift up one row. Your worksheet should look like this:

	A	B	C	D	E
1	**Title**		**WCS Cash Budget: 1992 Fiscal Year**		
2	**Created by**		Sam Bryan		
3					
4	**Budget Model Area**				
5				July	August
6			Gross Revenue		
7			Sales	$26,900	$26,900
8			Shipping	$5,550	$5,550
9			*Total*	**$32,450**	**$32,450**
11			Cost of Goods Sold		
12			Goods	$17,710	$17,710
13			Freight	$270	$270
14			Markdowns	$1,240	$1,240
15			Miscellaneous	$96	$96
16			*Total*	**$19,316**	**$19,316**
18			Gross Profit	**$13,134**	**$13,134**
20			Expenses		
21			Advertising	$4,000	$4,000
22			Salaries	$4,700	$4,700
23			Rent	$500	$500

Move the worksheet title and author left one cell

Now, move the worksheet title and author back to column B by deleting cells B1:B2.

1   Select cells B1:B2.

2   Choose Edit Delete.

✍   Press COMMAND+K.

3   Select the Shift Cells Left option.

4   Choose OK.

Your worksheet should look like this:

	A	B	C	D	E
1		Title	WCS Cash Budget: 1992 Fiscal Year		
2	Created by	Sam Bryan			
3					
4	Budget Model Area				
5				July	August
6			Gross Revenue		
7			Sales	$26,900	$26,900
8			Shipping	$5,550	$5,550
9			Total	$32,450	$32,450
11			Cost of Goods Sold		
12			Goods	$17,710	$17,710
13			Freight	$270	$270
14			Markdowns	$1,240	$1,240
15			Miscellaneous	$96	$96
16			Total	$19,316	$19,316
18			Gross Profit	$13,134	$13,134
20			Expenses		
21			Advertising	$4,000	$4,000
22			Salaries	$4,700	$4,700
23			Rent	$500	$500

Moving Cell Data

You use two commands together to move data—Edit Cut to cut selected data and Edit Paste to paste it into a new location. Unlike Edit Delete, Edit Cut does not physically remove a cell. Rather, it cuts the data within the cell so that you can paste it elsewhere.

Edit Cut and Edit Paste are used together to move cell data.

The Edit Cut command   Edit Cut defines the selection that will be moved when you choose the Edit Paste command. When you choose Edit Cut, your selected cells are surrounded by a moving dotted line called the marquee. Edit Cut has the keyboard shortcut COMMAND+X.

The Edit Paste command   Edit Paste pastes a selection that you defined with the Edit Cut or Edit Copy command into a new location. Edit Paste has the keyboard shortcut COMMAND+V.

You will find advantages to moving cells with two separate commands in Microsoft Excel. When you choose Edit Cut, the data you want to move is stored on the Clipboard. The cell data remains on the Clipboard until it is replaced by another cut or copied selection. You can do other tasks, such as opening another document, and then choose Edit Paste when you're ready to paste data into the other document.

Move a formula

Moving a formula doesn't change cell references.

Moving a formula is different from copying a formula. When you move a formula, the cell references still refer to the original cells. When you copy a formula, relative cell references adjust to the new location. Use Edit Cut and Edit Paste to move a formula.

1 Select cell D9.

2 Choose Edit Cut.

    ✍ Press COMMAND+X.

3 Select cell D4.

4 Choose Edit Paste.

    ✍ Press COMMAND+V.

The pasted formula, as displayed in the formula bar, did not change. It is still =SUM(D7:D8).

You can undo certain commands with Edit Undo.

The Edit Undo command   If you make a mistake or change your mind, you can reverse most commands and actions by choosing Edit Undo. The name of the Edit Undo command changes to reflect your last action. For example, if you find that you incorrectly pasted data in the worksheet, you can choose Edit Undo Paste, because Edit Paste was the last command chosen. Edit Undo has the keyboard shortcut COMMAND+Z.

Undo the last paste

To reverse your last editing change, you can use the Edit Undo Paste command. When you undo the paste, your cut selection is still defined. You can press COMMAND+PERIOD or ESC to cancel the marquee.

1 Choose Edit Undo Paste.

    ✍ Press COMMAND+Z.

2 Press COMMAND+PERIOD or ESC to cancel the marquee.

Copying to Nonadjacent Cells

You use Edit Copy and Edit Paste to copy cell data to other worksheet cells.

You already used the Edit Fill commands to copy cell contents into adjacent cells. When the cells you want to copy to are not next to the cells you want to copy from, you use two commands together: Edit Copy to define the data you want to copy, and Edit Paste to paste it into a new location.

The Edit Copy command   With Edit Copy, you define the selection that is copied to the Clipboard and will be pasted when you choose the Edit Paste command. Edit Copy has the keyboard shortcut COMMAND+C.

After you choose Edit Copy, you can choose Edit Paste as many times as you want.

The Edit Paste command   When you use Edit Copy and Edit Paste to copy cell data, the selection you defined remains in its original location and on the Clipboard. As long as the marquee is present, you can paste the selection from the Clipboard as many times as you want.

The Edit Insert Paste command   While Edit Paste replaces data in destination cells with the pasted data, Edit Insert Paste inserts cells to contain the pasted data and pastes the data in one step. As with Edit Paste, you can also use Edit Insert Paste to paste a selection from the Clipboard as many times as you want. After you choose Edit Cut or Edit Copy, the Edit Insert command changes to Edit Insert Paste.

In the next steps, you'll change the way budgeted insurance expenses are allocated over the year. To save on billing costs, the company will pay $236.50 twice a year, in July and January, rather than paying $43 a month.

Enter new insurance figures

First, change the budgeted insurance expenses for the first six months. The expense will be $236.50 for July and $0 for August through December. You can use the Edit Fill Right command to copy $0 from August to the next five months.

1 Select cell D25.

2 Type **236.50**

3 Press the RIGHT ARROW key.

   The number is displayed as $237 because of your number format.

4 In cell E25, type **0**

5 Click the enter box or press ENTER.

6 Select cells E25:I25.

7 Choose Edit Fill Right.

   ✎   Press COMMAND+R.

Copy the insurance figures to the second six months

The monthly insurance budget is the same for January through June as it is for July through December. Use the Edit Copy and Edit Paste commands to copy the figures from the first six months of the fiscal year to the second six months.

1   Select cells D25:I25.

2   Choose <u>E</u>dit <u>C</u>opy.

    ✍   Press COMMAND+C.

3   Select cell J25.

4   Choose <u>E</u>dit <u>P</u>aste.

    ✍   Press COMMAND+V. Or, you can just press ENTER (not RETURN) to paste the copy and cancel the marquee, because you won't be pasting another copy.

5   Press COMMAND+PERIOD or ESC to cancel the marquee.

Copying Cell Attributes Selectively

Sometimes you may want to copy only certain cell attributes, such as formulas, values, formats, or cell notes. You use the Edit Paste Special command to paste cell attributes selectively.

With Edit Paste Special, you can copy cell attributes selectively.

The Edit Paste Special command   With Edit Paste Special, you can paste certain attributes of the copy selection into the paste area. A dialog box appears in which you select the attribute you want to paste. You can also paste using an operation, such as addition or subtraction.

You will find many uses for Edit Paste Special. If you want to convert formulas into values, you can select Values in the Paste box. If you want to add a block of numbers to a similar block of numbers, you can select Add in the Operation box. Edit Paste Special is also useful for copying formats from one cell or cell range to another.

Turn on the Transpose check box to switch the orientation of data when you paste it.

Turn on the Skip Blanks check box if you don't want to paste blank cells contained in the copy selection. The Transpose check box pastes rows as columns and columns as rows.

In the next procedure, you'll use Edit Paste Special to copy the formats from column C to columns D through O to create identical border formats in those columns.

Copy the formats from column C to columns D through O

1 Select cells C6:C34.

2 Choose Edit Copy.

   ✐ Press COMMAND+C.

3 Select cells D6:O34.

4 Choose Edit Paste Special.

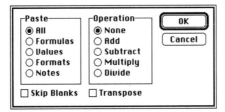

5 Under Paste, select the Formats option.

6 Choose OK.

When you pasted the border and shading formats, you also pasted the General number format from column C, replacing the dollar number format. You need to reformat the numbers and reapply the SumData style.

Reformat the numbers

1 Cells D6:O34 should still be selected.

2 Choose Format Number.

3 Select the first dollar number format: $#,##0_);($#,##0).

4 Choose OK.

5 Select cells D9:O9, D16:O16, D18:O18, D32:O32, and D34:O34.

6 In the style list on the tool bar, select SumData.

7 Scroll back to the beginning of the worksheet.

   ✐ Press COMMAND+HOME.

Your worksheet should look like this:

	A	B	C	D	E	
1		**Title WCS Cash Budget: 1992 Fiscal Year**				
2		**Created by** Sam Bryan				
3						
4		**Budget Model Area**				
5				July	August	
6			Gross Revenue			
7			Sales	$26,900	$26,900	
8			Shipping	$5,550	$5,550	
9			*Total*	*$32,450*	*$32,450*	
11			Cost of Goods Sold			
12			Goods	$17,710	$17,710	
13			Freight	$270	$270	
14			Markdowns	$1,240	$1,240	
15			Miscellaneous	$96	$96	
16			*Total*	*$19,316*	*$19,316*	
18			Gross Profit	$13,134	$13,134	
20			Expenses			
21			Advertising	$4,000	$4,000	
22			Salaries	$4,700	$4,700	
23			Rent	$500	$500	

Copy all cell attributes to column B

You'll create an indented look for your row titles by placing some of the titles in column B and some in column C. Use the Edit Fill Left command to copy the data in column C to column B.

1 Select cells B6:C34.

2 Choose Edit Fill Left. Remember to press SHIFT when you select the Edit menu.

Your worksheet should look like this:

	A	B	C	D	E
1		Title **WCS Cash Budget: 1992 Fiscal Year**			
2	**Created by** Sam Bryan				
3					
4	**Budget Model Area**				
5				July	August
6		Gross Reve	**Gross Revenue**		
7		Sales	Sales	$26,900	$26,900
8		Shipping	Shipping	$5,550	$5,550
9		*Total*	*Total*	**$32,450**	**$32,450**
11		Cost of Goo	**Cost of Goods Sold**		
12		Goods	Goods	$17,710	$17,710
13		Freight	Freight	$270	$270
14		Markdowns	Markdowns	$1,240	$1,240
15		Miscellaneou	Miscellaneous	$96	$96
16		*Total*	*Total*	**$19,316**	**$19,316**
18		Gross Profi	**Gross Profit**	**$13,134**	**$13,134**
20		**Expenses**	**Expenses**		
21		Advertising	Advertising	$4,000	$4,000
22		Salaries	Salaries	$4,700	$4,700
23		Rent	Rent	$500	$500

You need to clear the individual item titles from column B and the bold category titles from column C.

Clear the bold titles from column C

Clear the category and total titles from column C, leaving just the individual items. Then the bold titles in column B will spill into column C, hiding the vertical borders.

1 Select cells C6, C9, C11, C16, C18, C20, C32, and C34.

   ▣ For information on selecting multiple ranges, see Help. Choose Window Help, select Worksheet Procedures, and select the Making Multiple Selections topic.

2 Choose Edit Clear.

   ✎ Press COMMAND+B.

3 Choose OK.

Clear the individual item titles from column B

Clear everything but the bold titles from column B.

1 Select cells B7:B8, B12:B15, and B21:B31.

2 Choose Edit Clear.

3 Choose OK.

Insert a column

Insert a column at column B to separate the worksheet area titles from the data.

1   Select column B.

2   Choose Edit Insert.

    ✒   Press COMMAND+I.

Change column width for columns B and C

Change the width of columns B and C to make them each two characters wide.

1   Select columns B and C.

2   Drag the column C boundary left until "Width: 2:00" is displayed in the upper-left corner of the formula bar.

    ✒   Choose Format Column Width. In the Column Width box, type **2**. Choose OK.

Remove the right border in column C

You also copied the outline border format to column C. Remove the border between columns C and D to create one border around columns C and D.

1   Select cells C6:C34.

2   Choose Format Border.

3   Under Border, turn off the Right option.

4   Choose OK.

5   Select cells D6:D34.

6   Choose Format Border.

7   Turn off the Left option.

8   Choose OK.

Your worksheet should look like this:

	A	B	C	D	E	F	G
1			Title	WCS Cash Budget: 1992 Fiscal Year			
2			Created by	Sam Bryan			
3							
4			Budget Model Area				
5					July	August	Septe
6				Gross Revenue			
7				Sales	$26,900	$26,900	$2
8				Shipping	$5,550	$5,550	$
9				Total	$32,450	$32,450	$32
11				Cost of Goods Sold			
12				Goods	$17,710	$17,710	$1
13				Freight	$270	$270	
14				Markdowns	$1,240	$1,240	$
15				Miscellaneous	$96	$96	
16				Total	$19,316	$19,316	$19
18				Gross Profit	$13,134	$13,134	$13
20				Expenses			
21				Advertising	$4,000	$4,000	$
22				Salaries	$4,700	$4,700	$
23				Rent	$500	$500	

Save and close your worksheet

Before taking a break or continuing with the next lesson, save your work.

1 Choose File Save.

2 Choose File Close.

You Try It

In this lesson, you learned to copy and move cell data and formats. In the following exercise, you will practice the skills you learned.

The WCS copier advertising campaign will extend from July through September. The July expenses have already been entered in the worksheet. You need to modify the worksheet to reflect the following changes:

- Advertising is now divided into two expenses. Ad Production has a one-time budget of $75,000 and Periodical Advertising Space has a monthly budget of $25,000.

- Expenses for Clerical Support and General Administration will remain the same from July through September.

- Telemarketing expenses will occur in August, but not in September.

- Direct Mail expenses will occur in September, but not in August.

- An additional $50,000 will be allocated in August for the advertising campaign.

- Consulting expenses will occur in July only.

You can use the following steps as guidelines for modifying the worksheet.

1 Open the CAMPAIGN04 worksheet.

2 Save it as CAMPAIGN.

3 Use the Data Series command to label the columns for July through September in the Input and Budget Area of the worksheet.

4 Copy the cell data to the appropriate cells as previously described.

5 Use the Edit Copy and Edit Paste Special commands to copy the formatting from the July column to August and September.

6 Copy the formulas for adding Expenses and calculating Funds Remaining to August and September.

7 Change the Funds Remaining formula to reflect any additional budget allocations for August and September.

To see one possible result for this exercise, open CAMPAIGN04A. You can double-click any cell with a note marker for more information.

Summary and Preview

In this lesson, you learned to:

Copy data to adjacent cells   You used the Edit Fill commands to copy cell data and formulas to adjacent cells. Relative references in formulas copied to adjacent cells automatically adjust to calculate their new rows or columns.

Insert and delete rows, columns, and cells   You used the Edit Insert and Edit Delete commands to insert and delete cells and cell ranges.

Move cell data   You used the Edit Cut and Edit Paste commands to move cell data.

Undo a command   You used the Edit Undo command to reverse the Edit Paste command.

Copy data to nonadjacent cells   You used the Edit Copy and Edit Paste commands to copy cell data to nonadjacent cells.

Copy cell attributes selectively   You used the Edit Copy and Edit Paste Special commands to selectively paste attributes such as formatting.

In the next lesson, you'll write formulas to link information on one worksheet to another worksheet. You can use the linking capabilities of Microsoft Excel to work more flexibly. Instead of creating one large worksheet, you can create smaller, simpler worksheets that are linked together.

Linking Worksheets

░░

You will learn to:

- Write a formula that links one worksheet to another.
- Save and open a workspace file.

Estimated lesson time: 30 minutes

With Microsoft Excel, you can open multiple documents at the same time. You can also link worksheets.

In this lesson, you'll link one worksheet to another. You'll see how you can work efficiently with multiple documents. You'll also learn to save a group of documents as a workspace file so that you can open them all at once.

For more information on linking worksheets, see Chapter 8, "Working with Data from Multiple Documents," in the *Microsoft Excel User's Guide*.

Start the lesson

In this lesson, you'll work with a version of the BUDGET worksheet that has purpose and summary information added. The SALES HISTORY worksheet tracks the history of company sales and industry-wide sales. You will use these worksheets to learn more about linking.

1 Open the LESSON05A worksheet.

2 Choose File Save As.

3 In the Save Worksheet As box, type **BUDGET**

4 Choose the Save button.

   Choose the Yes button when you are asked if you want to replace the existing BUDGET worksheet.

5 Open the LESSON05B worksheet.

6 Choose File Save As.

7 In the Save Worksheet As box, type **SALES HISTORY**

8 Choose the Save button.

Arrange both windows

Use the Window Arrange All command to display both worksheets at the same time.

1 Close any other open windows.

2 Choose Window Arrange All.

Your screen should look like this:

Notes attached to cells A5 and A8 of the BUDGET worksheet contain information about the Purpose and Summary Areas and other worksheet changes. You can read cell notes by double-clicking any cell that has a note marker. A note marker appears as a dot in the upper-right corner of the cell.

Creating a Formula to Link One Worksheet to Another

Microsoft Excel recalculates a linking formula whenever you change the data it refers to.

Your BUDGET worksheet already contains the projected revenue data that you need in the SALES HISTORY worksheet. You'll create a formula that will link revenue data in the BUDGET worksheet to the SALES HISTORY worksheet.

External references   A linking formula contains an *external reference,* which is a reference to another document. An external reference consists of a document name and a cell reference, separated by an exclamation point. For example, you'll create a formula in SALES HISTORY that uses this external reference:

=BUDGET!$H$9

Create a linking formula

Because you can create a linking formula by pointing, it's as easy to create as any other formula. Create a formula in SALES HISTORY to total the projected monthly revenues from BUDGET.

1   On the SALES HISTORY worksheet, make sure cell D20 is selected.

2   Type an equal sign (=).

3   Switch to the BUDGET worksheet by clicking it.

    ✎   Choose Window BUDGET.

4   On the BUDGET worksheet, select cell H9.

5   Click the enter box or press ENTER.

Your screen should look like this:

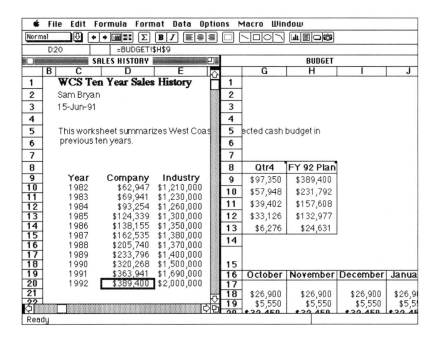

When you create a linking formula by pointing, Microsoft Excel uses absolute references. With absolute references, the formula will still refer to the same cells on the BUDGET worksheet if you copy the formula to another location on the SALES HISTORY worksheet.

The formula in SALES HISTORY depends on cells in BUDGET. The linking formula in SALES HISTORY returns an error value if you delete the BUDGET worksheet. SALES HISTORY is the *dependent worksheet* and BUDGET is the *supporting worksheet*.

Change the July budgeted sales revenues

Change the July projected sales revenues in BUDGET to see how changing your supporting worksheet affects your dependent worksheet.

1 Switch to the BUDGET worksheet by clicking it.

> ✐ Press COMMAND+M. If you have an extended keyboard, you can also press COMMAND+F6 to switch windows.

2 Select cell D18.

3 Type **27000**

4 Click the enter box or press ENTER.

The value in cell D20 on SALES HISTORY changes from $389,400 to $389,500.

Managing Links

You need to keep the dependent and supporting document relationship in mind as you create and use a system of linked worksheets. Here are some guidelines for managing links.

Saving linked worksheets   It's a good practice to save the supporting worksheet before saving the dependent worksheet. That way the correct names will be saved in the dependent worksheet when you quit Microsoft Excel. For example, if you change the name of the supporting worksheet, BUDGET, and later save the dependent worksheet, SALES HISTORY, the linking formulas in the dependent worksheet will contain the new name.

Moving linked worksheets with your operating system   If you use the Finder instead of Microsoft Excel to copy your dependent worksheet to a different disk or folder, you also need to copy the supporting worksheet.

The File Links command   If your links become disconnected, you can re-direct them with the File Links command. To redirect links to a supporting worksheet you've renamed or moved, open the dependent worksheet, choose File Links, choose the Change button, select the name of the supporting worksheet to which you want to redirect the links, and choose the Change button again.

Save and close the worksheet

Although the formula includes a reference to an external document, the BUDGET worksheet, the value in cell D20 of the SALES HISTORY worksheet remains the same.

As you close the BUDGET worksheet, watch the linking formula in the formula bar.

1 Choose File Save.

2 Choose File Close.

When you close the supporting document, your linking formula changes to show the supporting document's full pathname. When you open the BUDGET worksheet again, the formula changes back to show only the worksheet name.

Recently opened file list   If you have a large-screen Macintosh, the names of the last four files you opened are listed at the bottom of the File menu. You can reopen any of these files by choosing the filename from the list in the File menu.

If you have a 9-inch Macintosh screen, the recently opened file list isn't available. You need to choose File Open to reopen a file.

Reopen the worksheet

▶ Choose File BUDGET. Or choose File Open and select BUDGET.

Insert rows to move the Summary Area and its formulas

Just as references in formulas on the same worksheet are adjusted when you move the supporting cells, external references are adjusted. You will move the summary area along with its formulas by inserting rows into the worksheet.

1 On the BUDGET worksheet, select rows 8 through 10.

2 Choose Edit Insert.

3 Switch to the SALES HISTORY worksheet by clicking it.

    ✍ Press COMMAND+M.

The formula in cell D20 of the SALES HISTORY worksheet adjusts to display the new reference (BUDGET!$H$12) for the gross revenue formula. Whenever you move an absolute reference, such as $H$12, formulas in dependent cells automatically adjust to reflect the new location on the worksheet.

Saving a Workspace File

With a Microsoft Excel workspace file, you can save and open a group of documents at once rather than opening each document individually.

The File Save Workspace command   You can use File Save Workspace to save a *workspace*, which includes a list of the open documents, their position and arrangement, and their workspace settings. When you choose File Save Workspace, a dialog box appears so that you can name the workspace file.

Save the workspace

Now you will save a workspace file to use when you want to work with BUDGET and SALES HISTORY at the same time.

1 Choose File Save Workspace.

   ▢ To get Help on the File Save Workspace command, press COMMAND+SHIFT+QUESTION MARK while the File Save Workspace dialog box is displayed.

2 In the Save Workspace As box, type **BUDGET WORKSPACE**

3 Choose the Save button.

4 Choose the Yes button to save the changes in BUDGET.

5 Choose the Yes button to save the changes in SALES HISTORY.

Close the worksheets

1 Hold down SHIFT while you select the File menu.

   The Close command is replaced by the Close All command.

2 Choose File Close All.

Open a workspace file

Open the BUDGET WORKSPACE file. In later lessons you will open workspace files that have been created for you.

1 Choose File Open.

2 Select BUDGET WORKSPACE.

3 Choose the Open button.

The BUDGET and SALES HISTORY worksheets are displayed just as you saved them. Your screen should look like this:

Close the worksheets

1 Choose File Close All (remember to press the SHIFT key).

2 Choose the Yes button to save your changes in each worksheet.

You Try It

In the previous lessons, you created a worksheet to keep track of a three-month advertising budget. In this exercise you will link a worksheet detailing quarterly consulting expenses with a worksheet containing your advertising budget. You will link the Total Consulting Expenses cell on the CONSULT05 worksheet for July, August, and September with the Consultant's expense for those three months on the CAMPAIGN05 worksheet.

1 Open the UTRYIT05 WORKSPACE file to open CAMPAIGN05 and CONSULT05.

2 Arrange the windows so that CONSULT05 appears at the top of the screen and CAMPAIGN05 at the bottom.

3 On CAMPAIGN05, enter a formula for the July Consultant's Expense that links to the July Total Expenses cell on CONSULT05.

4 Create similar formulas for the August and September Consultant's Expenses cells that link to CONSULT05.

Your worksheets should look like this:

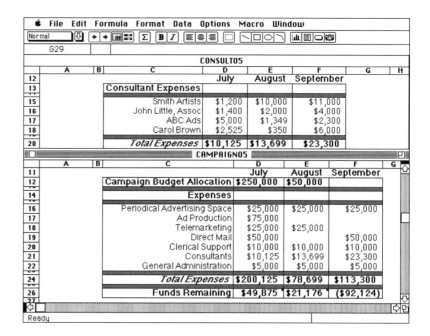

5 Close the worksheets when you are finished. Do not save the changes, because you may want to use these files again.

Summary and Preview

In this lesson, you learned to:

Write a formula that links one worksheet to another   You created a linking formula with an external reference by typing an equal sign (=) and then selecting a cell on another worksheet.

Save and open a workspace file   You used the File Save Workspace command to save a workspace file so that you can open a group of documents at the same time.

In the next lesson, you will create and use names in a worksheet. Names can help you to find areas of your worksheet quickly and easily and make your formulas easier to understand.

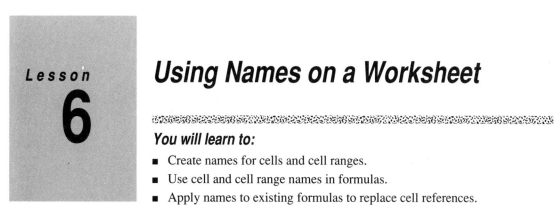

Using Names on a Worksheet

You will learn to:

- Create names for cells and cell ranges.
- Use cell and cell range names in formulas.
- Apply names to existing formulas to replace cell references.
- Name formulas containing relative references and constants.

Estimated lesson time: 45 minutes

With Microsoft Excel, you can name cells, cell ranges, and formulas.

In this lesson, you'll learn how to create and use names. You'll use names to simplify worksheet formulas and to define areas of the worksheet so you can find them easily. Using names will help you to create clear, easy-to-use, and well-documented worksheets.

For more information on defining and using names, see Chapter 6, "Organizing and Documenting a Worksheet," in the *Microsoft Excel User's Guide*.

Opening the Workspace File

You will continue to use the BUDGET and SALES HISTORY worksheets for this lesson. The worksheets are the same as those you were working with at the end of Lesson 5, except for the addition of an initial data area on the BUDGET worksheet. This data area contains variables for sales growth and cost of goods sold (COGS) increase, which you will use in worksheet formulas. You can open both worksheets at once by opening a workspace file.

Start the lesson

Open the workspace file that includes LESSON06A and LESSON06B.

▶ Open LESSON06 WORKSPACE.

Rename the LESSON06A worksheet

1 Switch to the LESSON06A worksheet.

Remember, you can switch to another open worksheet by clicking it with the mouse, by pressing COMMAND+M, or by selecting the name of the worksheet from the Window menu.

2 Choose File Save As.

3 Name the worksheet **BUDGET**

4 Choose the Save button.

5 When you are asked if you want to replace the existing BUDGET file, choose the Yes button.

Rename the LESSON06B worksheet

1 Switch to the LESSON06B worksheet.

2 Choose File Save As.

3 Name the worksheet **SALES HISTORY**

4 Choose the Save button.

5 When you are asked if you want to replace the existing file, choose the Yes button.

Your screen should look like this:

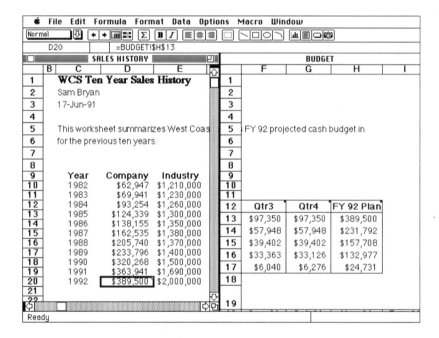

Cell D20 of the SALES HISTORY worksheet has a cell note attached which describes the linking formula you created in the previous lesson. You can double-click the cell to read the note.

Creating and Using Names

Names make your worksheets and formulas easier to update and understand. The following illustration shows how named worksheet ranges interrelate.

B	C	D	E	F	G	H
11						
12		Qtr1	Qtr2	Qtr3	Qtr4	FY 92 Plan
13	Gross Revenue	$97,450	$97,350	$97,350	$97,350	$389,500
14	Cost of Goods Sold	$57,948	$57,948	$57,948	$57,948	$231,792
15	Gross Profit	$39,502	$39,402	$39,402	$39,402	$157,708
16	Expenses	$33,363	$33,126	$33,363	$33,126	$132,977
17	Operating Income	$6,140	$6,276	$6,040	$6,276	$24,731
18						

These row titles are used as names...   ...in these formulas (=Gross_Profit–Expenses).

The Formula Define Name command   You can name a cell range, constant value, or formula with the Formula Define Name command. You can also change or delete an existing name with Formula Define Name.

Name the cell containing annual budgeted sales

Use the Formula Define Name command to assign the name "Total_Revenues" to the cell that contains your total revenues formula.

1 In the BUDGET worksheet, select cell H13.

2 Choose Formula Define Name.

    ◊ Press COMMAND+L.

3 In the Name box, type **Total_Revenues**

You must type an underline character between the words because names cannot contain spaces.

4 Choose OK.

With Formula Paste Name, you can easily find the name you want and paste it into your formula.

The Formula Paste Name command   You can use the Formula Paste Name command to paste a name into a formula you're creating. With Formula Paste Name, you can make sure that the name is defined and that it's spelled correctly in your formula.

Create a new linking formula using a name

You'll create a new linking formula that uses the name "Total_Revenues" rather than a cell reference. Instead of typing the formula, you will use the Formula Paste Name command.

1   Switch to the SALES HISTORY worksheet.

2   Select cell D20.

3   Type an equal sign (=) to begin a new formula.

4   Switch to the BUDGET worksheet.

5   Choose Formula Paste Name.

6   In the Paste Name box, select Total_Revenues.

7   Choose OK.

8   Click the enter box or press ENTER.

Your new formula appears in the formula bar. Your screen should look like this:

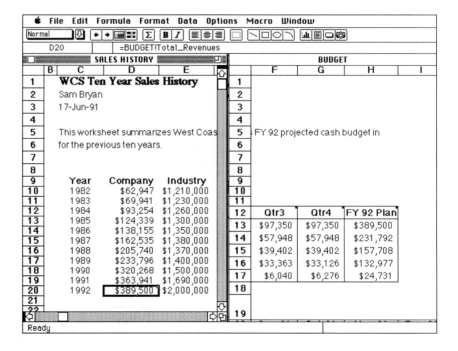

Enlarge the BUDGET worksheet window

For the rest of this lesson, you'll work only with the BUDGET worksheet. Close the SALES HISTORY worksheet and enlarge the BUDGET worksheet to fill the window.

1   Switch to the SALES HISTORY worksheet.

2   Choose File Close.

3   Choose the Yes button to save your changes.

4   In the upper-right corner of the BUDGET window, click the zoom box.

Use row and column titles to create names with Formula Create Names.

The Formula Create Names command   With Formula Create Names, you can define many names at once by using row and column titles as the names.

Create names in the Summary area

You'll use the row titles in the Summary Area to create names for Gross Revenue, Cost of Goods Sold, Gross Profit, Expenses, and Operating Income.

1   Select cells C13:G17.

2   Choose Formula Create Names.

3   Make sure the Left Column check box is turned on.

4   Choose OK.

If you want to see the names you created, choose Formula Define Name. Choose the Close button to close the dialog box.

Formula Apply Names makes it easy to apply names to formulas you've already written.

The Formula Apply Names command   Formula Apply Names replaces cell references in your formulas with the names you've created.

Apply names to the formulas in the Summary Area

You've already written formulas to total quarterly figures in the Summary Area of the worksheet. You will use the Formula Apply Names command to change cell references in these formulas to names. For example, the formula in cell H13 will change from =SUM(D13:G13) to =SUM(Gross_Revenue).

1   Select cells H13 through H17.

2   Choose Formula Apply Names.

   ▣   To get Help on the Formula Apply Names command, press COMMAND+SHIFT+QUESTION MARK while the Formula Apply Names dialog box is displayed.

3   Choose OK.

The formula bar shows the new formula in cell H13. Your screen should look like this:

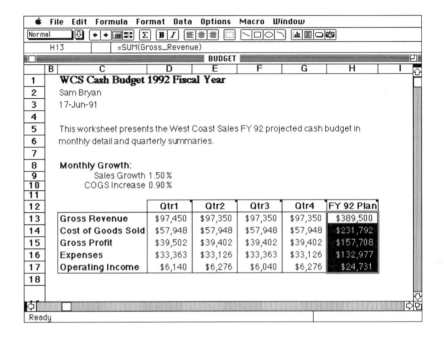

You can move to each cell in the range H13:H17 to see how names were applied to each formula.

Use names to find cell data

Use the Formula Goto command to find the intersection of two named areas.

You can use the Formula Goto command to find intersecting cells in named rows and columns. In this procedure, you will name the columns of quarterly data in the Summary Area and then use the Formula Goto command to find projected expenses for Qtr2.

1 Select cells D12:H17.

2 Choose Formula Create Names.

3 Make sure the Top Row check box is turned on.

4 Choose OK.

5 Choose Formula Goto.

   ✍ Press COMMAND+G.

6 In the Reference box, type **Qtr2 Expenses**

7 Choose OK.

Microsoft Excel selects cell E16, the cell containing the Qtr2 Expenses.

Naming Formulas and Values

The Formula Define Name and Formula Create Names commands can also be used to name a formula or a value. Using names is an easy way to create formulas.

Create names for the monthly growth variables

The variables Sales Growth and COGS Increase appear in the Initial Data Area. Sales Growth refers to a monthly growth rate of 1.50 percent and COGS Increase refers to a rate of 0.90 percent. You will name these variables and use them in worksheet formulas to project your budget.

Use the Formula Create Names command to name these new variables.

1 Select cells C9:D10.

2 Choose Formula Create Names.

3 Make sure the Left Column check box is turned on.

4 Choose OK.

Use the Sales Growth variable in a formula

Use the Sales Growth variable in a formula to forecast sales revenues. You'll enter the formula in the cell for August sales. Use July sales as the starting point for the rest of your calculations.

1 Select cell E22.

2 Type an equal sign (=).

3 Select cell D22.

4 Type *(1+

5 Choose Formula Paste Name.

6 Select Sales_Growth.

7 Choose OK.

8 Type)

9 Click the enter box or press ENTER.

The formula =D22*(1+Sales_Growth) appears in the formula bar.

You multiply 1+Sales_Growth by the previous month's sales rather than multiplying by the Sales_Growth variable and then adding the product to the previous month's total in a second formula.

Use Formula Define Name to name a formula.

Naming a formula   You can also name a formula with the Formula Define Name command. When the Formula Define Name dialog box appears, type the name in the Name box, type the formula in the Refers To box, and then choose the Add or OK button. The Add button adds the name to the list and leaves the dialog box open. The OK button adds the name to the list and closes the dialog box.

Name a formula for sales growth

You created a formula to calculate revenue growth based on a previous month's revenue projections. A formula, 1+Sales_Growth, automatically increases the previous month's sales projection. Use "Frm" to identify the name as a formula in the Formula Paste Name dialog box. You will give the name FrmSales_Growth to the formula 1+Sales_Growth.

1 Choose Formula Define Name.

   ✍ Press COMMAND+L.

2 In the Name box, type **FrmSales_Growth**

3 In the Refers To box, type **=1+Sales_Growth**

4 Choose OK.

Use the named formula to calculate shipping revenues

Replace the August Shipping revenue value with a formula. You will use the name FrmSales_Growth as part of this new formula.

1 Select cell E23.

2 Type **=d23***

3 Choose Formula Paste Name.

4 Select FrmSales_Growth.

5 Choose OK.

6 Click the enter box or press ENTER.

Cell E23 displays a new value, $5,633, reflecting a 1.50 percent increase over the previous month.

Copy the August shipping formula to the rest of the months

Use the Edit Fill Right command to copy the August Sales and Shipping revenue projection formulas to September through June.

1 Select cells E22:O23.

2 Choose Edit Fill Right.

The Summary Area data depends on the Budget Model Area data. A 1.50 percent growth rate in monthly shipping revenues results in a new projected Gross Revenue figure of $424,491 in cell H13. Your worksheet should look like this:

	B	C	D	E	F	G	H
8		Monthly Growth:					
9		Sales Growth 1.50%					
10		COGS Increase 0.90%					
11							
12			Qtr1	Qtr2	Qtr3	Qtr4	FY 92 Plan
13		Gross Revenue	$99,122	$103,650	$108,384	$113,335	$424,491
14		Cost of Goods Sold	$57,948	$57,948	$57,948	$57,948	$231,792
15		Gross Profit	$41,174	$45,702	$50,436	$55,387	$192,699
16		Expenses	$33,363	$33,126	$33,363	$33,126	$132,977
17		Operating Income	$7,812	$12,576	$17,074	$22,261	$59,722
18							
19							
20			July	August	September	October	November
21		Gross Revenue					
22		Sales	$27,000	$27,405	$27,816	$28,233	$28,657
23		Shipping	$5,550	$5,633	$5,718	$5,804	$5,891
24		Total	$32,550	$33,038	$33,534	$34,037	$34,547
26		Cost of Goods Sold					
27		Goods	$17,710	$17,710	$17,710	$17,710	$17,710
28		Freight	$270	$270	$270	$270	$270

Next, you will project the increases in cost of goods sold and variable expenses that go along with increasing revenues.

Name a formula for COGS growth

You will name a formula to use for projecting cost of goods sold and variable expenses for the 1992 fiscal year. This formula will add 1 to the COGS Increase rate and multiply the result by the previous month's value. The result of the formula includes the previous month's value plus the projected increase. You will create this formula the same way you created the formula to calculate sales growth.

1 Select cell E27.

2 Choose Formula Define Name.

   ✐ Press COMMAND+L.

3 In the Name box, type **FrmCOGS_Increase**

4 In the Refers To box, type **=1+COGS_Increase**

5 Choose OK.

The August Sales and Shipping formulas used cell references for the July Sales and Shipping formulas. Rather than using a cell reference, you can name a formula that acts as a reference.

Use Formula Define Name to name a formula that works as a relative reference.

Name a formula to act as a relative reference   With the Formula Define Name command, you can name a formula to act as a relative reference. This can help you clarify your formulas. Choose Formula Define Name, type the name in the Name box, and then type a relative cell reference in the Refers To box. For example, if the active cell is B1 and you want the name to refer to one cell to the left, type A1 in the Refers To box.

You can also point to cell A1 rather than typing the reference. If you enter a cell reference by pointing rather than by typing it, be sure to remove the dollar signs ($), either by editing the reference in the Refers To box or by using the Formula Reference command.

Name a relative reference

You will define a formula named PreviousMonth to refer to the data in the cell to the left of the formula. You will use PreviousMonth in formulas for projecting expenses.

1 Cell E27 should still be selected.

2 Choose Formula Define Name.

   ✐ Press COMMAND+L.

3 In the Name box, type **PreviousMonth**

4 In the Refers To box, type **=d27**

5 Choose OK.

Calculate August Goods costs

You will replace the August Goods value with a formula.

1 Cell E27, the August Goods value, should still be selected.

2 Type an equal sign (=).

3 Choose Fo_r_mula _P_aste Name.

4 In the Paste Name box, select PreviousMonth.

5 Choose OK to paste the name in the formula.

6 Type an asterisk (*).

7 Choose Fo_r_mula _P_aste Name.

8 Select FrmCOGS_Increase.

9 Choose OK to paste the name in the formula.

10 Click the enter box or press ENTER to enter the formula in the worksheet.

The formula bar displays the formula =PreviousMonth*FrmCOGS_Increase.

Copy the formula to Freight, Markdowns, and Miscellaneous

You will use the Edit Copy command to replace the other Cost of Goods Sold and variable expense values with the August Goods formula.

1 Cell E27, the August Goods formula, should still be selected.

2 Choose _E_dit _C_opy.

You can copy and paste cell data in many cells at once by selecting multiple ranges as the paste area.

3 Select cells E28:E30, E41, E44, and E46 (the remaining August variable expenses).

Remember to use the COMMAND key to make multiple selections.

4 Choose _E_dit _P_aste.

5 Press COMMAND+PERIOD or ESC to cancel the marquee.

The formula is copied to each of the selected cells. The formula replaces values and recalculates data based on the previous month's costs.

The remaining expenses are fixed expenses. You will replace each August fixed expense value with a formula that refers to the July fixed expense. By creating a formula that refers to a single cell, you can enter data once and have it automatically entered in any other dependent cells.

Create formulas for August fixed expenses

July fixed expenses will be allocated the same way for the remainder of the year. You will use the formula named PreviousMonth, which sets a cell's value to that of the previous month.

1   Select cell E36, the cell containing the August Advertising expense.

2   Type an equal sign (=).

3   Choose Formula Paste Name.

4   Select PreviousMonth.

5   Choose OK to paste the name in the formula.

6   Click the enter box or press ENTER to enter the formula in the worksheet.

7   Choose Edit Copy.

8   Select cells E37:E39, E42:E43, and E45.

9   Choose Edit Paste.

The copied formula is pasted in all the selected cells.

10   Press COMMAND+PERIOD or ESC to cancel the marquee.

Use a formula for January insurance

Change the January insurance expense to a formula.

1   Select cell J40.

2   Type an equal sign (=).

3   Select cell D40.

4   Click the enter box or press ENTER.

Copy the expense formulas through the rest of the fiscal year

You will copy the August Cost and Expense formulas to September through June.

1 Select cells E27:O30, E36:O39, and E41:O46.

2 Choose Edit Fill Right.

The Gross Revenue, Cost of Goods Sold, and Expense values are replaced by formulas. Your worksheet should look like this:

B	C	D	E	F	G	H
20		July	August	September	October	November
21	**Gross Revenue**					
22	Sales	$27,000	$27,405	$27,816	$28,233	$28,657
23	Shipping	$5,550	$5,633	$5,718	$5,804	$5,891
24	*Total*	$32,550	$33,038	$33,534	$34,037	$34,547
26	**Cost of Goods Sold**					
27	Goods	$17,710	$17,869	$18,030	$18,192	$18,356
28	Freight	$270	$272	$275	$277	$280
29	Markdowns	$1,240	$1,251	$1,262	$1,274	$1,285
30	Miscellaneous	$96	$97	$98	$99	$100
31	*Total*	$19,316	$19,490	$19,665	$19,842	$20,021
33	**Gross Profit**	$13,234	$13,548	$13,869	$14,195	$14,527
35	**Expenses**					
36	Advertising	$4,000	$4,000	$4,000	$4,000	$4,000
37	Salaries	$4,700	$4,700	$4,700	$4,700	$4,700
38	Rent	$500	$500	$500	$500	$500
39	Utilities	$75	$75	$75	$75	$75
40	Insurance	$237	$0	$0	$0	$0
41	Telephone and Telex	$280	$283	$285	$288	$290
42	Office Supplies	$147	$147	$147	$147	$147
43	Training	$100	$100	$100	$100	$100
44	Travel and Entertainment	$200	$202	$204	$205	$207
45	Taxes and Licenses	$240	$240	$240	$240	$240
46	Interest	$800	$807	$814	$822	$829
47	*Total*	$11,279	$11,054	$11,065	$11,077	$11,089
49	**Operating Income**	$1,956	$2,495	$2,803	$3,118	$3,438

Save and close the worksheet

Save and close the worksheet. If you want to continue with the "You Try It" exercise, you will use another version of the BUDGET worksheet.

1 Choose File Save.

2 Choose File Close to close the worksheet.

You Try It

Now you will complete the BUDGET worksheet using what you have learned. Open the LESSON06C worksheet and rename it BUDGET. The worksheet now includes additions to the Initial Data Area for entry of initial Revenue, COGS, and Expense data. The Initial Data Area also includes variables for monthly Sales Growth and COGS Increase.

To complete the worksheet, you need to copy the data from July Revenue, COGS, and Expenses to their respective categories in the Initial Data Area; create names for each of the initial data categories; and then replace the July budget values with formulas that refer to each budget category in the Initial Data Area. You will use the names for the categories in the Initial Data Area in the July formulas.

1 Open the LESSON06C worksheet.

2 Save the worksheet as **BUDGET**

 Choose the Yes button to replace the existing BUDGET worksheet.

3 Copy the July Revenue, COGS, and Expense values to their corresponding budget categories in the Initial Data Area. Use Edit Paste Special and select the Values option.

4 Use the Formula Create Names command to create a name for each budget category in the Initial Data Area.

5 Use any method to replace the July Revenue, COGS, and Expense values with formulas that refer to the same categories in the Initial Data Area.

6 You can change any of the Initial Data Area values, including monthly sales growth and COGS increase, to project different budget scenarios.

 To see a possible solution to this exercise, open LESSON06D.

7 Save and close the worksheets when you are finished.

Summary and Preview

In this lesson, you learned to:

Create names for cells and cell ranges   You created several names at once with the Formula Create Names command.

Use cell and cell range names in formulas   You used names in place of cell references to make formulas easier to use.

Apply names to existing formulas to replace cell references   You used the Formula Apply Names command to replace existing cell references in formulas with names.

Name formulas containing relative references and constants   You used the Formula Define Name command to create a formula to use as a constant and another to use as a reference. These named formulas helped to simplify your worksheet formulas.

In the next lesson, you will learn about worksheet outlining and data consolidation. With these powerful Microsoft Excel features, you can easily analyze and summarize your data.

Worksheet Outlining and Data Consolidation

You will learn to:

- Create an outline on a worksheet.
- Expand and collapse an outline.
- Format a group of worksheets at the same time.
- Consolidate data from different worksheets.

Estimated lesson time: 45 minutes

With Microsoft Excel, you can outline a worksheet. You can also edit a group of worksheets together and consolidate data from several sources.

In this lesson, you'll use three powerful Microsoft Excel features: worksheet outlining, workgroup editing, and data consolidation. With outlining, you can view your data in summary or detail. Workgroup editing is useful for setting up and formatting a group of worksheets in preparation for consolidating data. Data consolidation provides an easy method of summarizing the data on several worksheets into one worksheet.

The worksheets in this lesson examine the number of employees and payroll costs for the three divisions of West Coast Sales. Each division includes marketing, engineering, research and development, and administrative departments.

In the first part of this lesson, you'll use a worksheet that breaks down personnel statistics within each division by department. Then you'll format a group of worksheets containing personnel statistics for each division. You'll consolidate the data in these worksheets by department so that you can compare the total costs of administration, marketing, engineering, and research and development throughout the company.

For more information on	See in the *Microsoft Excel User's Guide*
Worksheet outlining	Chapter 6, "Organizing and Documenting a Worksheet"
Consolidating data Workgroup editing and formatting	Chapter 8, "Working with Data from Multiple Documents"

Start the lesson

Open the LESSON07 worksheet and rename it WCS DIVISION. You'll create an outline on this worksheet and examine the data in different ways by switching between summary and detail views.

1 Open LESSON07.

2 Save the worksheet as **WCS DIVISION**

Understanding a Worksheet Outline

You can outline your worksheet with up to seven levels of information. Outlining a worksheet differs from outlining a text document such as a report or a proposal. In a text document, the subordinate information appears below a heading. When you outline a worksheet, subordinate information typically appears above or to the left of the summary information. A worksheet can be outlined horizontally by rows and vertically by columns, depending on how the summary formulas are calculated.

Creating a Worksheet Outline

You can create an outline on a new or existing worksheet. To create an outline, you must write your formulas so that references consistently point in one direction, such as rows always referring up and columns always referring left. You can have only one outline at a time on a worksheet.

The Formula Outline command   You can use the Formula Outline command to create a worksheet outline. Select the cell range to be outlined, choose Formula Outline, and then choose the Create button. Under Direction, you can indicate the direction of your formulas. You can also apply styles consistently to your worksheets by turning on the Automatic Styles check box.

Create a worksheet outline

Use the Formula Outline command to outline the Personnel Cost Data area on the WCS DIVISION worksheet. Create both horizontal and vertical outlines of the data.

1 Select rows 9 through 24.

2 Choose Formula Outline.

> ❓ To get Help on the Formula Outline command, press COMMAND+ SHIFT+QUESTION MARK while the Formula Outline dialog box is displayed.

The check boxes are already turned on for Automatic Styles, Summary Rows Below Detail, and Summary Columns To Right Of Detail.

3   Choose the Create button.

Outline symbols appear to the left of the row headings.

4   Select columns D through H.

5   Choose Formula Outline.

6   Choose the Create button.

Outline symbols appear above the row headings.

Your worksheet should look like this:

			Number of			Personnel
9	C	Department	Employees	Payroll	Benefits	Costs
10	Copier Division	Marketing	4	$177,000	$53,100	$230,100
11		Engineering	7	$303,500	$91,050	$394,550
12		R and D	2	$98,000	$29,400	$127,400
13		Administrative	4	$160,000	$48,000	$208,000
14		Copier Total	17	$738,500	$221,550	$960,050
15	Fax Division	Marketing	2	$105,000	$31,500	$136,500
16		Engineering	6	$250,500	$75,150	$325,650
17		R and D	2	$97,000	$29,100	$126,100
18		Administrative	3	$132,000	$39,600	$171,600
19		Fax Total	13	$584,500	$175,350	$759,850
20	Printer Division	Marketing	7	$320,500	$96,150	$416,650
21		Engineering	14	$655,000	$196,500	$851,500
22		R and D	5	$214,000	$64,200	$278,200
23		Administrative	4	$179,000	$53,700	$232,700
24		Printer Total	30	$1,368,500	$410,550	$1,779,050
25						
26						

Row level buttons

Column level buttons

Column level bar

Collapse button

Row level bar

Expand button   Expands (displays) the hidden subordinate data.

Collapse button   Collapses (hides) the rows or columns enclosed by the row or column level bar.

Row and column level buttons   Display specified levels of data. For example, in an outline with three levels of data, clicking the 2 button displays information for the first two levels.

Row and column level bars   Show the hierarchy of the levels of data. To hide the detail rows and columns, click the collapse button on the level bar.

Collapse the outline to level 1

Now that you've outlined the worksheet, view the division summaries.

1 Click the row level 1 button.

Your worksheet should look like this:

	C	D	E	F	G	H
			Number of			Personnel
9		Department	Employees	Payroll	Benefits	Costs
14		Copier Total	17	$738,500	$221,550	$960,050
19		Fax Total	13	$584,500	$175,350	$759,850
24		Printer Total	30	$1,368,500	$410,550	$1,779,050
25						

Expand button

2 Click the column level 1 button.

Your worksheet should look like this:

	C	D	E	H
			Number of	Personnel
9		Department	Employees	Costs
14		Copier Total	17	$960,050
19		Fax Total	13	$759,850
24		Printer Total	30	$1,779,050
25				

Some of the outlining controls are on the tool bar. The following illustration shows the location of the outlining buttons on the tool bar.

Demote button | | Show outline symbols button

Promote button | | Select visible cells button

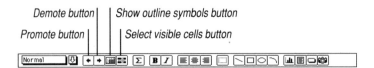

Promote button Promotes selected rows or columns to a higher level in the outline.

Demote button Demotes selected rows or columns to a more subordinate level in the outline.

Show outline symbols button Displays or hides the outline symbols on your worksheet.

Select visible cells button Selects only the visible cells when the outline is collapsed. You can work with the visible cells to plot a chart or copy only a specific level of information.

Demote the columns

The Number of Employees column is not part of your outline because the summary formulas in column H don't refer to the data in column E. If you select the column and click the demote button, it will become level 2 data in your worksheet. Once you have demoted the Number of Employees column, demote the Payroll and Benefits columns to level 3.

1 Select column E.

2 On the tool bar, click the demote button.

Press COMMAND+SHIFT+K to demote a row or a column in an outline.

   ✑   Press COMMAND+SHIFT+K.

3 Click the expand button above column H to expand the outline.

4 Select columns F and G.

5 On the tool bar, click the demote button.

   ✑   Press COMMAND+SHIFT+K.

The outline symbols for the columns reflect your changes. Your worksheet should look like this:

		C	D	E	F	G	H
	9		Department	Number of Employees	Payroll	Benefits	Personnel Costs
	14		Copier Total	17	$738,500	$221,550	$960,050
	19		Fax Total	13	$584,500	$175,350	$759,850
	24		Printer Total	30	$1,368,500	$410,550	$1,779,050
	25						

Collapse and expand the outline

Now that you've changed the column levels, view the level 1 and level 2 columns with the level 1 rows.

1 Click the column level 2 button.

   Your worksheet should look like this:

		C	D	E	H
	8				
	9		Department	Number of Employees	Personnel Costs
	14		Copier Total	17	$960,050
	19		Fax Total	13	$759,850
	24		Printer Total	30	$1,779,050
	25				

2 Click the expand buttons to see the detail.

Remove the outline

To remove the outline, select the rows or columns and promote them until the outline symbols disappear.

1 Select rows 9 through 24.

2 Click the promote button until the outline symbols disappear.

3 Select columns D through H.

4 Click the promote button until the outline symbols disappear.

If you just want to turn off the display of outline symbols, click the show outline symbols button on the tool bar.

Save and close the worksheet

In the remainder of this lesson, you will work with a different group of worksheets that contain the same data. Save and close the WCS DIVISION worksheet.

1 Choose File Save.

2 Choose File Close.

Formatting a Workgroup

With Microsoft Excel, you can save time by entering data and editing, formatting, and changing display options in several worksheets at the same time. You do this by defining similar worksheets as a *workgroup*. Any changes you make in the active worksheet are duplicated in all the sheets in the workgroup.

Open the workspace

The LESSON07 WORKSPACE contains the WCS DEPARTMENTS07, FAX07, COPIER07, and PRINTER07 worksheets. You will format these worksheets as a workgroup and then consolidate their data into one worksheet.

▶ Open LESSON07 WORKSPACE.

Rename the worksheets

Change the names of the worksheets to WCS DEPARTMENTS, FAX, COPIER, and PRINTER.

1 With the WCS DEPARTMENTS07 worksheet active, choose File Save As.

2 In the Save Worksheet As box, select and delete the "07" from the worksheet name.

3 Choose the Save button.

You'll remove the "07" from each of the other worksheet names.

4 Repeat steps 1 through 3 for each of the worksheets, renaming them PRINTER, FAX, and COPIER.

5 Switch to WCS DEPARTMENTS.

Your screen should look like this:

	A	B	C	D	E	F	G	H
			PRINTER					
			FAX					
			COPIER					
			WCS DEPARTMENTS					
1	Title		WCS Personnel by Department Within Divisions					
2								
3	Purpose		Use this worksheet to consolidate data from the Copier, Fax,					
4			and Printer Division personnel worksheets.					
5								
6	Initial Data		Benefit Cost	30%				
7								
8	WCS Personnel Data by Department							
9								
10			Department	Number of Employees	Payroll	Benefits	Personnel Costs	
11			Marketing					
12			Engineering					
13			R and D					
14			Administrative					
15			Total Personnel	0	$0	$0	$0	

Use the workgroup commands to work with several worksheets at once.

The Window Workgroup command   You can use the Window Workgroup command to group several worksheets for formatting, editing, or data entry. Working with a workgroup is useful for preparing your worksheets for operations such as data consolidation.

The Edit Fill Workgroup command   You can use the Edit Fill Workgroup command to copy the contents of a cell in the active sheet to the other worksheets.

Create a workgroup

You'll create a workgroup to format all of the open worksheets at once.

1 With the WCS DEPARTMENTS worksheet active, choose Window Workgroup.

2 The names of the four worksheets should be selected. If not, hold down COMMAND and click the name of each worksheet.

3 Choose OK.

The word "[Workgroup]" appears after the worksheet name in each title bar.

Format the workgroup

You will format all of the worksheets at one time by formatting the active worksheet. Format the row and column heads.

1 Select cells C10:C15 and D10:G10.

2 In the style list on the tool bar, select the Heading style.

3 Select cells D10:G10.

4 Choose Format Column Width.

5 Choose the Best Fit button.

6 Select cells C10:C15.

7 Click the right alignment button in the tool bar.

Your worksheet should look like this:

	A	B	C	D	E	F	G	H
			PRINTER [Workgroup]					
			FAX [Workgroup]					
			COPIER [Workgroup]					
			WCS DEPARTMENTS [Workgroup]					
1	Title		WCS Personnel by Department Within Divisions					
2								
3	Purpose		Use this worksheet to consolidate data from the Copier, Fax, and					
4			Printer Division personnel worksheets.					
5								
6	Initial Data		Benefit Cost	30%				
7								
8	WCS Personnel Data by Department							
9								
10			Department	Number of Employees	Payroll	Benefits	Personnel Costs	
11			Marketing					
12			Engineering					
13			R and D					
14			Administrative					
15			Total Personnel	0	$0	$0	$0	

End the group editing session

You are finished working with the workgroup. To dissolve the workgroup, switch to another worksheet. You can either click another worksheet window or choose the name of another worksheet from the Window menu.

▶ Switch to the COPIER worksheet.

The worksheets are no longer part of a workgroup. You can now work with each worksheet individually.

Consolidating Data from Multiple Worksheets

You can use consolidation to summarize large amounts of data. When you choose the Data Consolidate command, Microsoft Excel consolidates the source ranges you specify.

The Data Consolidate command   You can use the Data Consolidate command to summarize data from several *source* areas into a *destination* area. You can use 11 different functions, including AVERAGE, COUNT, MAX, and SUM, to consolidate data into the destination area. Unless you specify another function, Microsoft Excel uses the SUM function for consolidating data.

Consolidating by category of data   You consolidate data by category when the source areas are in different locations but include similar data. To consolidate by category, you turn on the Top Row or Left Column check box. You can also turn on both check boxes.

Consolidating by position of data   You consolidate data by position when the source areas are in worksheets created from identical templates. For example, individual expense reports created from the same template can be consolidated by position into a destination worksheet.

You can create links to your source data and outline the destination worksheet to view the summary or detail data.

Creating links to source data   You can create links to source data by choosing Data Consolidate and turning on the Create Links To Source Data check box. When you create links to source data, Microsoft Excel creates a linking formula for each cell, inserting rows and columns in your destination area to hold the linking formulas. Microsoft Excel creates an outline and subordinates the source data references in the destination area. Make sure that the inserted columns and rows for the linked source data do not disrupt other parts of your worksheet.

Consolidate the data by department

With the WCS DEPARTMENTS worksheet active, you'll choose the Data Consolidate command and define source areas for consolidation on the COPIER, FAX, and PRINTER worksheets.

1 Switch to the WCS DEPARTMENTS worksheet.

2 Select cells C10:G14.

3 Choose Data Consolidate.

> ⚡ To get Help on the Data Consolidate command, press COMMAND+ SHIFT+QUESTION MARK while the Data Consolidate dialog box is displayed.

4 Move to the Reference box.

5 With the Data Consolidate dialog box still open, choose <u>W</u>indow PRINTER.

6 Select cells C10:G14. You can scroll to see the cells, and you can drag the dialog box by the title bar if it is in your way.

In the Reference box, PRINTER!$C$10:$G$14 appears.

7 Choose the Add button.

8 Repeat steps 5 through 7 for the COPIER and FAX worksheets.

9 Turn on the Top Row and Left Column check boxes.

10 Turn on the Create Links To Source Data check box.

11 Choose OK.

You can select cells C10:G27 and use the Format Column Width command so that you can see all of your data. Your worksheet should look like this:

1 2		C	D	E	F	G	H	I
	10	Department		Number of Employees	Payroll	Benefits	Personnel Costs	
⊞	14	Marketing		13	$602,500	$180,750	$783,250	
⊞	18	Engineering		27	$1,209,000	$362,700	$1,571,700	
⊞	22	R and D		9	$409,000	$122,700	$531,700	
⊞	26	Administrative		11	$471,000	$141,300	$612,300	
	27	Total Personnel		60	$2,691,500	$807,450	$3,498,950	
	28							

You created links to the source worksheets. Microsoft Excel consolidated the data in the source areas, inserted references to the source data, and created an outline.

Expand the outline

Expand the outline to examine the detail.

▶ Click the row level 2 button.

Notice that rows 11, 12, and 13 took on the formatting of the previous row. Format these rows to look like the following illustration:

	C	D	E	F	G	H
			Number of			
10	Department		Employees	Payroll	Benefits	Personnel C
11		COPIER	4	$177,000	$53,100	$230,100
12		FAX	2	$105,000	$31,500	$136,500
13		PRINTER	7	$320,500	$96,150	$416,650
14	Marketing		13	$602,500	$180,750	$783,250
15		COPIER	7	$303,500	$91,050	$394,550
16		FAX	6	$250,500	$75,150	$325,650
17		PRINTER	14	$655,000	$196,500	$851,500
18	Engineering		27	$1,209,000	$362,700	$1,571,700
19		COPIER	2	$98,000	$29,400	$127,400
20		FAX	2	$97,000	$29,100	$126,100
21		PRINTER	5	$214,000	$64,200	$278,200
22	R and D		9	$409,000	$122,700	$531,700
23		COPIER	4	$160,000	$48,000	$208,000
24		FAX	3	$132,000	$39,600	$171,600
25		PRINTER	4	$179,000	$53,700	$232,700
26	Administrative		11	$471,000	$141,300	$612,300
27	Total Personnel		60	$2,691,500	$807,450	$3,498,950
28						

Save and close the worksheets

1 Choose File Close All.

Remember to hold down SHIFT to choose File Close All.

2 Choose the Yes button to save your changes in each worksheet.

You Try It

West Coast Sales issues a consolidated sales report for all products from its two sales regions. Open the SALES REPORT07, NORTH07, and SOUTH07 worksheets with the UTRYIT07 WORKSPACE.

Rename the worksheets with the File Save As command, removing the "07" from each name. Use the Window Workgroup command to create a workgroup; then format the source worksheets. Consolidate the products sold onto the SALES REPORT worksheet. Create links to the source data and view the resulting outline.

1 Open UTRYIT07 WORKSPACE.

2 Rename each worksheet. The worksheet names should be SALES REPORT, NORTH, and SOUTH.

3 Create a workgroup containing the SALES REPORT, NORTH, and SOUTH worksheets.

4 Select cells C13:E13.

5 In the style list on the tool bar, select the Heading style.

6 Dissolve the workgroup and switch to SALES REPORT.

7   Select cells C13:E24.

8   Choose Data Consolidate.

9   Select cells C13:E20 on the NORTH and SOUTH worksheets. Turn on the Top Row and Left Column check boxes.

10   Choose OK.

The SALES REPORT worksheet should look like this:

	A	B	C	D	E	F
11	Sales Data		Company-Wide Sales Fiscal Year 1992 Qtr 2			
12						
13			Product	Units Sold	Revenues (in thousands)	
14			Compact Printer	39,000	$9,750	
15			Impact Printer	52,500	$7,875	
16			Laser Printer	17,000	$25,500	
17			XL 150 Copier	12,500	$11,875	
18			XL 225 Copier	11,000	$16,500	
19			XL 500 Copier	9,000	$19,800	
20			XL 700 Printer	5,000	$25,000	
21			Letter Printer	23,000	$5,750	
22			XL 100 Copier	13,000	$11,310	
23			XL 250 Copier	15,000	$26,250	
24			XL 300 Copier	11,000	$19,250	

Save and close the worksheets when you are finished.

Summary and Preview

In this lesson, you learned to:

Create an outline on a worksheet   You created an outline by selecting an area of a worksheet and using the Format Outline command.

Expand and collapse an outline   You used the outline buttons to expand and collapse an outline.

Format a group of worksheets at the same time   You created a workgroup with the Window Workgroup command and then formatted all the sheets in the workgroup at once.

Consolidate data from different worksheets   You used the Data Consolidate command to consolidate data from source worksheets into a destination worksheet.

The next lesson offers an overview of additional useful worksheet features.

Advanced Worksheet Features

You will learn to:

- Use array formulas.
- Create a conditional formula with the IF function.
- Solve "what-if" problems using goal seeking.
- Use custom functions to automate frequently used formulas.
- Protect cells and objects.
- Hide and unhide documents.

Estimated lesson time: 25 minutes

In this lesson, instead of going through step-by-step procedures, you will examine sample documents to learn about advanced worksheet features including arrays, goal seeking, custom functions, and the IF function. By trying out the online examples, you'll know what features are available in Microsoft Excel and where to look when you want to use them in your work.

For more information on	See
Array formulas Goal seeking	Chapter 7, "Analyzing and Calculating a Worksheet," in the *Microsoft Excel User's Guide*
Custom functions	Chapter 17, "Creating and Using Custom Worksheet Functions," in the *Microsoft Excel User's Guide*
IF function	IF function in the *Microsoft Excel Function Reference*

Start the lesson

The LESSON08 WORKSPACE file opens the documents INTRODUCTION08, ARRAYS08, GOAL SEEK08, IF_FUNCTION08, CUSTOM FUNCTION08 MACROS, and CUSTOM FUNCTION08 WORKSHEET. It also opens a hidden macro sheet, LESSON08 MACROS. You can test the examples in these documents while reading about these advanced Microsoft Excel features.

▶ Open LESSON08 WORKSPACE.

The INTRODUCTION08 worksheet appears. Your screen should look like this:

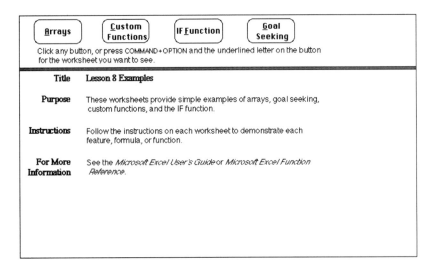

You'll use the buttons at the top of the worksheet to display the examples while you read about them.

Annotating a Worksheet

You can attach notes to cells with Formula Note.

The Formula Note command   Use the Formula Note command to attach a cell note to a cell. Notes do not appear in the cell, but can be printed with the worksheet or viewed with the Formula Note or Window Show Info command. Cells with notes attached are indicated by a note marker in the upper-right corner, as you've seen in previous lessons. Adding a note to a cell is useful for documenting assumptions, "footnoting" the source of your cell data, or explaining a formula.

Text boxes   If you want additional information to appear right on your worksheet, create a text box with the text box tool and type the information you want in the box. In the sample documents, text boxes contain information about each worksheet or macro sheet. Text boxes can be moved, sized, attached to cells, or sized with cells. You can format the text within each box with multiple fonts, styles, and sizes. You'll learn more about text boxes in Lesson 16, "Using Embedded Charts and Worksheet Graphics."

You can customize your worksheet by assigning buttons to macros.

Buttons   You can create a button on your worksheet with the button tool and then use the button to run a command macro. Buttons, like text boxes, can be moved, resized, attached to cells, or sized with cells. You can type a name in the button and change the font, style, and size of the button name. You'll learn more about buttons in Lesson 17, "Recording Macros."

Using the buttons   Clicking a button at the top of each sample worksheet activates a different worksheet. You can also press COMMAND+OPTION and the underlined letter in each button.

Click the Arrays button

You'll click the Arrays button to switch to the ARRAYS08 worksheet.

▶ Click the Arrays button.

✎   Press COMMAND+OPTION+A.

The ARRAYS08 worksheet becomes the active sheet.

Improving Your Analysis

You can use arrays to write multiple-value formulas and improve worksheet efficiency.

Array formulas and functions   With arrays, you can build formulas that produce multiple results or that operate on a range of cells. An array formula occupies only one cell but can calculate values in many cells in which you need to do similar calculations. You can greatly improve the efficiency of your worksheet by using array formulas instead of ordinary, single-value formulas.

Some Microsoft Excel functions are array functions. For example, to perform regression analysis in Microsoft Excel, you use the TREND, GROWTH, LINEST, and LOGEST array functions.

Edit the array formula

This example demonstrates how to use an array formula to multiply and add a group of cells in one formula, rather than using separate formulas to multiply price by units and then sum the total cost of all units.

1   Follow the instructions on the worksheet to edit the formula.

2   When you've completed your entry, press COMMAND+ENTER.

The total cost of the fleet of cars and trucks, $219,000, appears in cell E14.

Formulas with IF functions   You can use the IF function to build a conditional formula. It will return one value if the conditions are true and another value if the conditions are false. The IF function can be used to apply different formulas based upon its conditions. For example, a payroll worksheet can use an IF function to calculate sales bonuses depending on monthly sales.

The auto-sum button   You can click the auto-sum button in the tool bar to paste the SUM function and a proposed cell range into the active cell. With the keyboard, press COMMAND+SHIFT+T. Click the button again or press ENTER to accept the proposed range and cancel the marquee.

Build a formula with the IF function

The example uses an IF function to calculate bonuses based on the salesperson's commissions. If the commissions are less than $5,000, the salesperson receives no bonus. If the commissions are $5,000 or greater, the salesperson receives an additional 10 percent.

1 At the top of the ARRAYS08 worksheet, click the IF Function button to switch to the IF_FUNCTION08 worksheet.

   ✍ Press COMMAND+OPTION+F.

2 Follow the instructions on the worksheet to edit and copy the formula.

After the formula evaluates the conditions, C. Tyler receives "No Bonus" and S. Bryan receives a bonus of $750.

The Formula Goal Seek command   You can use the Formula Goal Seek command to find the values a formula needs to reach a value that you specify. For example, you can afford a loan payment of $250 a month and want to find the maximum principal amount you can borrow. Goal seeking is useful for solving many "what-if" problems.

Find a monthly loan payment

This example uses the Formula Goal Seek command to find how much money you can borrow if your maximum payment is $250 per month and the annual interest rate is 10 percent.

1 At the top of the IF_FUNCTION08 worksheet, click the Goal Seeking button to switch to the GOAL SEEK08 worksheet.

   ✍ Press COMMAND+OPTION+G.

2 Follow the instructions on the worksheet to use Formula Goal Seek.

The Principal cell changes to display the maximum loan amount, $11,766. If you choose OK in the Goal Seek dialog box, this value is entered on the worksheet.

Custom functions   You can write your own custom functions to automate specialized calculations that you perform often. You create a custom function on a macro sheet by specifying the function's arguments, its formula, and the values it returns. Once you define and name a custom function, you can use it as you would any worksheet function, such as SUM. The custom function appears in the Formula Paste Function dialog box whenever the macro sheet is open.

Use a custom function in a formula

First you will look at CUSTOM FUNCTION08 MACROS, where the FAHRENHEIT and CELSIUS custom functions are defined. Then you will switch to the CUSTOM FUNCTION08 WORKSHEET, where the functions are used.

1   At the top of the GOAL SEEK08 worksheet, click the Custom Functions button to switch to CUSTOM FUNCTION08 MACROS.

   ✍   Press COMMAND+OPTION+C.

2   Examine the custom functions. Every custom function has these three parts: the arguments, the formula, and the value returned. The accompanying comments explain how this custom function is written.

3   At the right side of CUSTOM FUNCTION08 MACROS, click the Custom Function Worksheet button.

   ✍   Press COMMAND+OPTION+W.

4   Follow the instructions on the worksheet to edit and use the formulas.

The initial data is the boiling point for Fahrenheit and Celsius. The formulas convert the initial data from Fahrenheit to Celsius and vice versa. You can change the initial data to test the conversion formulas.

Protecting a Worksheet

You can protect cells and objects from being edited.

The Format Cell Protection and Object Protection commands   With Format Cell Protection and Format Object Protection, you can protect data in the selected cells or objects such as text boxes, buttons, and charts from being edited or displayed in the formula bar.

You can use a password to protect a worksheet.

The Options Protect and Unprotect Document commands   With Options Protect Document, you can turn on cell protection. You can also protect the worksheet window so that it can't be sized or closed. To protect the worksheet, you type a password. Be sure you don't lose your password, or you won't be able to reverse protection of the worksheet. To unprotect a worksheet, choose the Options Unprotect Document command and type your password.

Unprotect a worksheet

The sample worksheets are protected, except for the cells where you will enter data. No password was used to protect the documents, so you can protect and unprotect them.

1   On the CUSTOM FUNCTION08 WORKSHEET, select any cell other than those you edited and try to enter data.

   The message, "Locked cells cannot be changed," is displayed.

2   Choose the Options Unprotect Document command.

You can now change the data in any cell or object on the worksheet.

You can hide a worksheet with Window Hide.

The Window Hide and Window Unhide commands   With Window Hide, you can hide the active window. With Window Unhide, you can unhide a hidden window. Hiding windows is useful when you want a document to be open but not visible. A hidden window is closed when you choose the File Close All command. To close only the hidden window, you need to unhide the window and then choose the File Close command.

Unhide a macro sheet

The hidden LESSON08 MACROS macro sheet contains the macros you ran when you clicked the buttons on the sample documents. Unhide the macro sheet window.

1 Choose Window Unhide.

2 Select LESSON08 MACROS.

3 Choose OK.

> The LESSON08 MACROS macro sheet appears on your screen.

Close the sample documents

Close all the documents, but do not save the changes.

1 Choose File Close All.

> Remember to press SHIFT to choose File Close All.

2 Choose the No button when you are asked if you want to save your changes.

Summary and Preview

In this lesson, you learned to:

Use array formulas   You used an array formula to calculate the cost of a fleet of cars and trucks.

Create a conditional formula with the IF function   You used an IF function to calculate bonuses based on commissions.

Solve "what-if" problems using goal seeking   You used the Formula Goal Seek command to find how much you could borrow for a certain monthly payment.

Use custom functions to automate frequently used formulas   You used custom functions to convert Fahrenheit to Celsius and vice versa.

Protect cells and objects   You used the Options Unprotect Document command to remove document protection from a worksheet.

Hide and unhide documents   You used the Window Unhide command to unhide a macro sheet.

The next lesson describes setting up your printer to print with Microsoft Excel.

3 Printing

Lesson 9

Installing and Setting Up Your Printer

You will learn to:

■ Select a printer.

Estimated lesson time: 15 minutes

In this lesson, you'll learn how to specify a printer for use with Microsoft Excel. You should go through this lesson if you are unfamiliar with selecting a printer.

For more information on installing your printer, see Chapter 15, "Printing," in the *Microsoft Excel User's Guide*, and your Macintosh documentation.

Selecting a New Printer

Your printer configuration applies to your Macintosh environment and all Macintosh applications, not just Microsoft Excel.

On the Macintosh, you use the Chooser to change printers for all of your applications.

The Chooser   Select a printer with the Chooser, a desk accessory that you can run while using Microsoft Excel. Select Chooser from the Apple menu, click the icon for the printer you want, and then, if necessary, click the icon for the printer port (printer or modem) to which the printer is attached.

Using the Chooser desk accessory is a convenient way to change printers, because you can make the changes without leaving Microsoft Excel.

Open the Chooser from the Apple menu

▶ Choose the Chooser from the Apple menu ( ) in the upper-left corner of the Microsoft Excel window.

The Chooser dialog box looks like this:

Select a new printer

1 Click the LaserWriter or ImageWriter icon.

2 If you are printing on an ImageWriter printer, click the icon for the port (printer or modem) to which the printer is attached.

   If you are on an AppleTalk network, select the AppleTalk zone and then the name of the printer.

Close the Chooser

▶ Click the close box to close the Chooser.

Summary and Preview

In this lesson, you learned to:

Select a printer   You used the Chooser desk accessory to select a printer.

In the next lesson, you will print the BUDGET worksheet. You will add a header to the printed pages, specify print titles for every page, specify which portions of the worksheet to print, and preview the pages before printing.

Setting Up the Page and Printing

You will learn to:

- Preview a printed worksheet.
- Set up the page layout.
- Print part of a worksheet.
- Specify titles to be printed on every page.

Estimated lesson time: 25 minutes

In this lesson, you'll print the BUDGET worksheet. First, you'll preview the worksheet to see how it would look if you printed it right away. Then you'll change the page layout, add a header to the page, specify what part of the worksheet you want to print, and then specify titles to be printed on every page. After you make these changes, you'll preview the worksheet again before printing it.

For more information on setting up your pages, see Chapter 15, "Printing," in the *Microsoft Excel User's Guide*.

Start the lesson

Open LESSON10 and rename it BUDGET.

1 Open LESSON10.

2 Save the file as **BUDGET**

3 Choose the Yes button to replace the existing BUDGET file.

Arrange the worksheet window

1 Close any other open windows.

2 Choose <u>W</u>indow <u>A</u>rrange All.

Setting Up the Document for Printing

The File Page Setup command   With File Page Setup, you can specify settings such as paper orientation (vertical or horizontal), paper size, and special printer effects. You can also add headers and footers, change margins, and turn off gridlines and row and column headings so they aren't printed.

Your File Page Setup settings are saved with the document. Use File Page Setup again when you want to make a change.

Change the paper orientation

If you print the BUDGET worksheet horizontally (in landscape orientation), you can print more columns per page. Change the paper orientation with the File Page Setup command.

1 Choose File Page Setup.

> ⚙ To get Help on the File Page Setup command, press COMMAND+ SHIFT+QUESTION MARK while the File Page Setup dialog box is displayed.

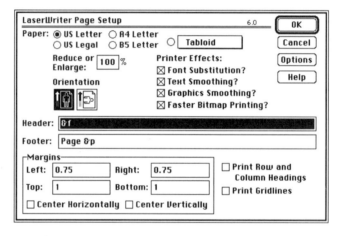

2 Under Orientation, select the landscape (horizontal) option.

3 Choose OK.

Previewing the Printed Worksheet

You can preview your worksheet on the screen to see how it will look when you print it. By previewing your worksheet first, you can save time and trips to the printer.

Microsoft Excel automatically prints the entire worksheet. You can also choose to print a range of cells.

The File Print Preview command   With File Print Preview, you can preview a document as it will look when printed. You can change some settings, such as margin and column width, in the preview window. Then you can print the document or return to your document window without printing. You can also preview a document by choosing File Print and turning on the Print Preview check box.

Preview the printed page

You can preview a printed worksheet with File Print Preview.

Preview the BUDGET worksheet to see how it would look if you printed it now.

▶ Choose File Print Preview.

Your worksheet should look like this:

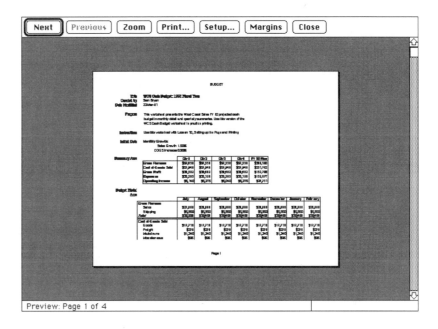

Your worksheet may look slightly different, depending on the printer you have selected. File Print Preview uses the fonts available with your printer.

The Print Preview window   You can use the Zoom, Next, and Previous buttons to look at a part of the page in detail or move to other pages. When you point to the page, the mouse pointer turns into a magnifier. You can click the page with the magnifier to enlarge the page to actual-size view and click again to reduce it to the full-page view. Choose the Setup button to change headers, footers, or other settings in the File Page Setup dialog box. When you choose the Margins button, the margins and columns appear on your document. You can change margins and column width by dragging the handles.

Close the preview window

Close the preview window when you are ready to return to the regular worksheet window.

▶ Choose the Close button.

Setting Up the Page Layout

By default, Microsoft Excel uses the filename as the page header and the page number as the page footer. You'll create a custom page header and include special codes to format the header.

Change the header

1 Choose File Page Setup.

2 In the Header box, type **&c&bWest Coast Sales: FY 1992 Projected Budget**

The code "&c" centers the header and the code "&b" makes the header bold.

3 Choose OK.

The Options Set Print Area command   With Options Set Print Area, you can identify the area of the worksheet you want to print. If you don't set a print area, Microsoft Excel prints all of the worksheet that contains data. You can also define a multiple selection as the print area.

When you set a print area, Microsoft Excel names your selection Print_Area. To delete the print area, you can choose Formula Define Name, select Print_Area, and then choose the Delete button.

Instead of printing the entire worksheet, you will print only the Budget Model Area.

Select an area of the worksheet to print

Now identify the part of the worksheet you want to print.

1   Select cells A22:O52.

Remember that you can use Formula Goto to select a cell range.

2   Choose Options Set Print Area.

The Options Set Print Titles command   With Options Set Print Titles, you can designate row titles and column titles to be printed on each page. The rows you use for column titles or the columns you use for row titles can be anywhere on the worksheet, but the row titles are printed at the left of a page and the column titles are printed at the top of a page. If your print titles are within the print area, they will only appear once on the page where they first occur.

When you set print titles, Microsoft Excel names your selection Print_Titles. To delete the print titles, you can choose Formula Define Name, select Print_Titles, and then choose the Delete button.

Set columns A, B, and C as the titles for each page

Because all of the Budget Model Area rows fit on one printed page but the columns are printed over two pages, you need to set the row titles to be printed on each page. Set columns A, B, and C as the print titles for each page. When you set print titles, you must select the entire row or column.

1   Select columns A, B, and C.

2   Choose Options Set Print Titles.

Printing a Worksheet

Now that you've specified how you want the BUDGET worksheet to be printed, you can choose the File Print command.

The File Print command   Use File Print to print your document. In the File Print dialog box, you can specify the number of copies and pages to print. You can turn on the Print Preview check box to display print preview. You can also print the cell notes alone or with the worksheet.

Preview and print the worksheet

Preview your worksheet once again before printing it.

1 Choose File Print.

✐ Press COMMAND+P.

2 Turn on the Print Preview check box.

3 Choose OK.

4 Choose the Zoom button or click the worksheet with the magnifier.

Your worksheet should look like this:

| Next | Previous | Zoom | Print... | Setup... | Margins | Close |

Budget Model
Area

	July	August	September	October	November	December	January
Gross Revenue							
Sales	$27,000	$27,405	$27,816	$28,233	$28,657	$29,087	$29,523
Shipping	$5,550	$5,633	$5,718	$5,804	$5,891	$5,979	$6,069
Total	$32,550	$33,038	$33,534	$34,037	$34,547	$35,066	$35,592
Cost of Goods Sold							
Goods	$17,710	$17,869	$18,030	$18,192	$18,356	$18,521	$18,686
Freight	$270	$272	$275	$277	$280	$282	$285
Markdowns	$1,240	$1,251	$1,262	$1,274	$1,285	$1,297	$1,308
Miscellaneous	$96	$97	$98	$99	$100	$100	$10
Total	$19,316	$19,490	$19,665	$19,842	$20,021	$20,201	$20,383
Gross Profit	$13,234	$13,548	$13,869	$14,195	$14,527	$14,865	$15,209
Expenses							
Advertising	$4,000	$4,000	$4,000	$4,000	$4,000	$4,000	$4,000
Salaries	$4,700	$4,700	$4,700	$4,700	$4,700	$4,700	$4,700
Rent	$500	$500	$500	$500	$500	$500	$500
Utilities	$75	$75	$75	$75	$75	$75	$75
Insurance	$237	$0	$0	$0	$0	$0	$237
Telephone and Telex	$280	$283	$285	$288	$290	$293	$295
Office Supplies	$147	$147	$147	$147	$147	$147	$147
Training	$100	$100	$100	$100	$100	$100	$100
Travel and Entertainment	$200	$202	$204	$205	$207	$209	$21
Taxes and Licenses	$240	$240	$240	$240	$240	$240	$240
Interest	$800	$807	$814	$822	$829	$837	$844
Total	$11,279	$11,054	$11,065	$11,077	$11,089	$11,101	$11,349
Operating Income	$1,956	$2,495	$2,803	$3,118	$3,438	$3,764	$3,86

Preview: Page 1 of 2

5 Choose the Next button to see the rest of the worksheet.

6 Choose the Print button.

Save and close the worksheet

The BUDGET worksheet is complete, so you'll save and close the worksheet. Your page setup settings are saved with the worksheet.

1 Choose File Save.

2 Choose File Close.

Printing a Chart

Printing a chart is similar to printing a worksheet, except that a chart is always printed on a single page. Also, when a chart is the active document, some options in the File Page Setup dialog box are different.

If you have a one-color printer, you may want to use the Format Patterns command to change patterns for the data series. That way, you'll be better able to distinguish the different data series. You will learn more about formatting charts in Lesson 14, "Formatting a Chart."

Printing Worksheet Data and a Chart Together

If you want to print worksheet data and a chart on the same page, you can use the chart tool on the tool bar to create a chart right on the worksheet. You will learn more about embedding charts in worksheets in Lesson 13, "Creating a Chart."

Summary and Preview

In this lesson, you learned to:

Preview a printed worksheet   You used the File Print Preview command to preview a worksheet before printing it.

Set up the page layout   You used the File Page Setup command to change the headers on your page and the paper orientation for your printed worksheet.

Print part of a worksheet   You used the Options Set Print Area command to specify a section of a worksheet to be printed.

Specify titles to be printed on every page   You used the Options Set Print Titles command to specify row titles to be printed on each page.

In the next part of this book, you'll learn about Microsoft Excel databases. You can set up a database on your worksheet and use it for analyzing your worksheet data. In the next lesson, you will define a database on a worksheet and use the data form to find, add, and delete records.

4

Using Worksheet Databases

Setting Up a Database on Your Worksheet

You will learn to:

- Define a database on a worksheet.
- Use the data form to add and change database records.
- Sort data in a database.
- Use the data form to set criteria for selecting database records.
- Use criteria to find database records.
- Delete database records.

Estimated lesson time: 40 minutes

In this lesson, you'll learn how to set up and use a database to help manage and analyze data on your worksheet.

For more information on creating databases and using the data form, see Chapter 9, "Creating and Using a Database on a Worksheet," in the *Microsoft Excel User's Guide*.

Start the lesson

Open the LESSON11 WORKSPACE file. This workspace includes COPY RECORDS11 and LESSON11, which you will rename PERSONNEL. You will create a worksheet database on PERSONNEL and then copy records to it from COPY RECORDS.

1 Open LESSON11 WORKSPACE.

2 The LESSON11 worksheet should be active.

3 Save the worksheet as **PERSONNEL**

Setting Up a Database

You can use a database on your worksheet as a tool to organize, update, retrieve, analyze, and summarize large amounts of information. Microsoft Excel worksheet databases are organized in a tabular form. Each row is a *record* of information and each column is a *field* of information common to all records. The first row of the database contains the *field names*.

Field names

	C	D	E	F	G	H
13	Last Name	First Name	Position	Department	Salary	Start Date
14	Albert	Max	Group Assist.	Marketing	$21,888	8/16/89
15	Aruda	Felice	Admin. Assist.	Admin	$22,341	3/19/85
16	Beech	Susan	Senior Engineer	Engineering	$56,854	9/13/84
17	Coyne	Dennis	Software Engineer	Engineering	$39,812	10/15/86
18	Davison	Karen	Unit Mgr.	Admin	$77,305	3/4/78
19	Farley	Sam	Group Mgr.	Marketing	$67,512	6/12/80
20	Fein	Caroline	Engineering Mgr.	Engineering	$71,563	7/5/82
21	Goldberg	Malcolm	Product Marketer	Marketing	$43,222	4/29/87
22	Johnson	Miguel	Senior Engineer	Engineering	$54,898	5/19/86
23	Lempert	Alexandra	Research Scientist	R and D	$41,225	9/18/88
24	Raye	Alice	Group Assist.	Engineering	$23,998	12/10/89
25	Richards	Phillip	Cost Accountant	Admin	$39,875	4/22/88
26	Sargent	Evelyn	Product Marketer	Marketing	$46,096	2/23/85
27	Solomon	Ari	Technician	Engineering	$27,543	11/14/89
28	Wells	Jason	Admin Assist.	Admin	$24,512	2/26/84
29	White	Jessica	Mechanical Engineer	Engineering	$37,888	10/20/87
30						

Record

Once you have organized your database, you can use it to:

- Find and extract records from the database based on criteria you define.
- Analyze data statistically.
- Sort data alphabetically or numerically, by rows or columns, in ascending or descending order.
- Print data organized for specific purposes.

Planning the database   Before you create your database, plan it carefully. Start by thinking about the reports you will need to generate from the data. For example, a report might include a list of employee earnings and commissions. Next, decide what type of records you will keep. Each record contains information about a single person or event. For example, you may keep a record of each sale. You could use these records to generate the report on earned commissions.

Creating the fields   Once you decide what type of reports and records you will need, create fields for the categories of data you need for the report. Make sure to create fields for the smallest units of data you will be analyzing. For example, rather than a Name field, you could include separate fields for First Name and Last Name. Then you could generate a sales report listing sales personnel by last name and create a form letter addressing each salesperson by first name.

Calculated fields   You can create fields that calculate values based on the data in other fields. For example, rather than entering the amount of tax withheld, you can enter a formula that will calculate the tax withheld based on gross wages.

In this lesson, you will create a database of personnel records for the WCS Copier Division. You will use this database to add, change, find, sort, and delete records.

Enter the field names

Start setting up the database by entering field names.

1   On the PERSONNEL worksheet, select cells C22:H22.

2   Type the field names as shown in the following illustration. The first one has already been entered for you.

	C	D	E	F	G	H
22	Last Name	First Name	Position	Department	Salary	Start Date
23						

Format the field names

You will format the field names so that you can distinguish them from the database records you will be entering.

▶   In the style box on the tool bar, select the Heading style.

Enter a database record

You can enter records in a database just as you enter any other data on a worksheet, or you can use the data form. Later in this lesson you will use the data form to enter records in the worksheet. Enter the first record by selecting cells and typing the information.

1   Select cells C23:H23.

2   Type the record as shown in the following illustration.

	C	D	E	F	G	H
22	Last Name	First Name	Position	Department	Salary	Start Date
23	Price	David	Chief Scientist	R and D	$57,963	1/9/76
24						

The Data Set Database command   You define the range of cells you want to use as a database with the Data Set Database command. Select a cell range that includes the field names and any data records you've entered; then choose Data Set Database. Microsoft Excel names your selection "Database."

Define the worksheet database

Now that you have entered the field names and one data record, use the Data Set Database command to define this range as a database.

1   Select cells C22:H24.

   You include a blank row after the last record so that you can add more records without redefining the database.

2   Choose Data Set Database.

Copy records from another worksheet

To save time, you will copy the remaining personnel records from the COPY RECORDS worksheet.

1   Switch to the COPY RECORDS worksheet.

2   Select cells C14:H29.

3   Choose Edit Copy.

4   Switch to the PERSONNEL worksheet.

5   Select cell C24.

6   Choose Edit Insert Paste.

7   Choose OK.

With the Edit Insert Paste command, you can paste and insert the copied records at the same time. Because you included a blank record when you defined the database, the database expands to accommodate the pasted records.

Format the database

1   If necessary, use the Format Number command to format cell G23 for dollars.

2   Use the Format Column Width command to widen any columns that are too narrow.

Using the Data Form

You can update a database with the data form.

The Data Form command   You use the Data Form command to display a dialog box in which you can add, change, find, or delete records. The dialog box is arranged as a data entry form for the defined database. When you add or delete records in the data form, Microsoft Excel adjusts the range named Database.

Use the data form to enter a record

1 Choose the Data Form command.

   ☐ To get Help on the Data Form command, press COMMAND+SHIFT+ QUESTION MARK while the Data Form dialog box is displayed.

2 Choose the New button to display a blank new record.

3 Type the information shown in the illustration in all the fields in the data form. After each entry, click the next field or press TAB.

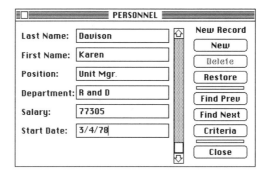

4 Press ENTER to add the record and leave the data form open.

When you add a record by using the data form, Microsoft Excel expands the range named Database to include the new record.

Edit the database with the data form

You can also edit or delete records with the data form. Use the data form to correct the spelling of Caroline Fine's last name.

1 In the data form, use the scroll bar to scroll through the records until Caroline Fein's record appears in the data form.

   ✐ Press the UP or DOWN ARROW key until the record is displayed.

2 In the Last Name box, type **Fine**

3 Choose the Close button.

The new spelling is reflected in the database range of the worksheet.

Sorting a Database

The Data Sort command   You can use the Data Sort command to sort database records by up to three fields. Microsoft Excel sorts the selected records in ascending or descending order according to the contents of a key column, or field, within the selection. You can also use the Data Sort command whenever you need to sort worksheet data by row or column.

Make sure to sort only the database records. Do not include the field names in a sort.

You sort database records by first selecting the range to be sorted. Make sure you select only the records and not the field names; otherwise the field names will be sorted along with the records. Choose the Data Sort command, specify the sort key (the field you want to sort by), and then choose the Sort button.

You can sort by three key fields of data at a time. All data is sorted by the first key. The second key sorts records that have identical information in the first key, and the third key sorts records that have identical information in the first two keys.

For example, a three-key sort by department, last name, and first name would sort all records first by department, then by last name within each department, and finally by first name for employees with the same last name.

	C	D	E	F	G	H	I
13	Last Name	First Name	Positions	Department	Salary	Start Date	
14	Aruda	Felice	Admin. Assist.	Admin	$22,341	3/19/85	
15	Richards	Phillip	Cost Accountant	Admin	$39,875	4/22/88	
16	Wells	Jason	Admin. Assist.	Admin	$24,512	2/26/84	
17	Beech	Dennis	Software Engineer	Engineering	$39,812	10/15/86	
18	Beech	Susan	Senior Engineer	Engineering	$56,854	9/13/84	
19	Fine	Caroline	Engineering Mgr	Engineering	$71,563	7/5/82	

Sort a worksheet database

You can use the Edit Undo command to undo a sort.

You will use the Data Sort command to sort the database records. Be sure to include all columns with fields of data; otherwise the selected fields will be separated from the fields that were not selected. If you make a mistake, use the Edit Undo command to undo the sort.

1 On the PERSONNEL worksheet, select cells C23:H40.

2 Choose Data Sort.

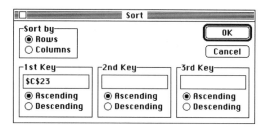

3 To enter the first key, select any cell in column C, the Last Name field.

✎ In the 1st Key box, type the reference of any cell in column C, the Last Name field.

4 Choose OK.

The records are sorted by last name in ascending order (from A through Z). Your worksheet should look like this:

	C	D	E	F	G	H
22	Last Name	First Name	Position	Department	Salary	Start Date
23	Albert	Max	Group Assist.	Marketing	$21,888	8/16/89
24	Aruda	Felice	Admin. Assist.	Admin	$22,341	3/19/85
25	Beech	Susan	Senior Engineer	Engineering	$56,854	9/13/84
26	Coyne	Dennis	Software Engineer	Engineering	$39,812	10/15/86
27	Davison	Karen	Unit Mgr.	R and D	$77,305	3/4/78
28	Farley	Sam	Group Mgr.	Marketing	$67,512	6/12/80
29	Fine	Caroline	Engineering Mgr.	Engineering	$71,563	7/5/82
30	Goldberg	Malcolm	Product Marketer	Marketing	$43,222	4/29/87
31	Johnson	Miguel	Senior Engineer	Engineering	$54,898	5/19/86
32	Lempert	Alexandra	Research Scientist	R and D	$41,225	9/18/88
33	Price	David	Chief Scientist	R and D	$57,963	1/9/76
34	Raye	Alice	Group Assist.	Engineering	$23,998	12/10/89
35	Raye	Alice	Group Assist.	Engineering	$23,998	12/10/89
36	Richards	Phillip	Cost Accountant	Admin	$39,875	4/22/88
37	Sargent	Evelyn	Product Marketer	Marketing	$46,096	2/23/85
38	Solomon	Ari	Technician	Engineering	$27,543	11/14/89
39	Wells	Jason	Admin Assist.	Admin	$24,512	2/26/84
40	White	Jessica	Mechanical Engineer	Engineering	$37,888	10/20/87
41						

If you will need to return the records to the order in which they were entered, set up the database with an additional field containing a date or number. Sort by this field to return the records to their original sequence.

Sort the records by two key fields

You can use the Data Sort command to organize the records in different ways. You will now sort the data by department. Within each department employee records will be sorted in descending order by salary. Employees with the highest salaries within each department will be listed first.

1 Cells C23:H40 should still be selected.

2 Choose Data Sort.

3 To enter the first key, select any cell in column F, the Department field.

    ✍ In the 1st Key box, type the reference of any cell in column F.

4 To enter the second key, move to the 2nd Key box and select any cell in column G, the Salary field.

    ✍ In the 2nd Key box, type the reference of any cell in column G.

5 Under 2nd Key, select the Descending option.

6 Choose OK.

The records are sorted in descending order by salary within each department. Your worksheet should look like this:

	C	D	E	F	G	H
22	Last Name	First Name	Position	Department	Salary	Start Date
23	Richards	Phillip	Cost Accountant	Admin	$39,875	4/22/88
24	Wells	Jason	Admin. Assist.	Admin	$24,512	2/26/84
25	Aruda	Felice	Admin. Assist.	Admin	$22,341	3/19/85
26	Fine	Caroline	Engineering Mgr.	Engineering	$71,563	7/5/82
27	Beech	Susan	Senior Engineer	Engineering	$56,854	9/13/84
28	Johnson	Miguel	Senior Engineer	Engineering	$54,898	5/19/86
29	Coyne	Dennis	Software Engineer	Engineering	$39,812	10/15/86
30	White	Jessica	Mechanical Engineer	Engineering	$37,888	10/20/87
31	Solomon	Ari	Technician	Engineering	$27,543	11/14/89
32	Raye	Alice	Group Assist.	Engineering	$23,998	12/10/89
33	Raye	Alice	Group Assist.	Engineering	$23,998	12/10/89
34	Farley	Sam	Group Mgr.	Marketing	$67,512	6/12/80
35	Sargent	Evelyn	Product Marketer	Marketing	$46,096	2/23/85
36	Goldberg	Malcolm	Product Marketer	Marketing	$43,222	4/29/87
37	Albert	Max	Group Assist.	Marketing	$21,888	8/16/89
38	Davison	Karen	Unit Mgr.	R and D	$77,305	3/4/78
39	Price	David	Chief Scientist	R and D	$57,963	1/9/76
40	Lempert	Alexandra	Research Scientist	R and D	$41,225	9/18/88

If you have a large number of records to sort, you can define a name that refers to database records but not field names. Then you can use the Formula Goto command to select the records before sorting.

Finding and Deleting Database Records

You can find individual records in your database according to *criteria* that you set. You can set criteria with the data form or with the Data Set Criteria command. You will use the Data Set Criteria command in Lesson 12 to set criteria on the worksheet. In the next procedure, you will use the data form to set criteria and find records.

Setting criteria and finding data with the data form   You set criteria by displaying the data form, choosing the Criteria button, and then typing your criteria in the field name boxes. Press ENTER to display the first record that matches your criteria. Choose the Find Prev or Find Next button to display additional records matching your criteria in the data form.

Comparison criteria   You can set comparison criteria to find records that match or fall within the limits you specify. You can enter text strings to match records exactly or use a combination of text strings and operators to set criteria. You can use the following operators:

Operator	Meaning
=	Equal to
>	Greater than
<	Less than
>=	Greater than or equal to
<=	Less than or equal to
<>	Not equal to

To find records in the PERSONNEL database, you would enter the following comparison criteria in the data form:

To find	Type
All Marketing Department employees	**Marketing** in the Department box
All employees with salaries greater than $40,000	**>40000** in the Salary box
All employees with salaries less than $50,000	**<50000** in the Salary box
All employees who started on or after 1/1/86	**>=1/1/86** in the Start Date box
All employees who started on or before 4/5/85	**<=4/5/85** in the Start Date box
All employees except for those in the Administrative Department	**<>Admin** in the Department box

Delete records

A duplicate of Alice Raye's record appears in the worksheet database. You will find and delete the duplicate record.

1 Choose Data Form.

2 Choose the Criteria button.

3 In the Last Name box, type **Raye**

4 Press ENTER.

The record for Alice Raye appears in the data form.

5 Choose the Find Next button.

The duplicate record is displayed. Alice Raye's records are numbered 10 of 18 and 11 of 18.

6 Choose the Delete button.

A message warns you that the record will be permanently deleted. Deletions cannot be undone.

7 Choose OK.

The duplicate record is deleted.

Find records

Find the records for all employees who started working before 1985.

1   Choose the Criteria button.

2   Press DELETE to delete "Raye" from the Last Name box.

3   In the Start Date field, type **<1/1/1985** to find all the employees who started before January 1, 1985.

4   Press ENTER.

The record for Karen Davison appears in the data form.

5   Choose the Find Next button until you hear a beep.

This means that the last record is reached. Microsoft Excel starts finding records where it left off after the last search, in which you deleted a duplicate record for Alice Raye. You need to choose Find Prev to view the records at the beginning of the database.

6   Choose the Find Prev button until you've seen all the matching records.

7   Choose the Close button to close the data form.

Save and close the worksheets

Save and close the worksheets. You will use different worksheets for the "You Try It" exercise.

1   Choose File Save.

2   Choose File Close All.

Remember to hold down the SHIFT key to choose File Close All.

You Try It

The UTRYIT11 worksheet contains the personnel records for the WCS Printer Division. In this exercise, you will rename the worksheet, define the database, add a record, edit a record, find records, sort the records, and print the database.

1   Open the UTRYIT11 worksheet and rename it **PRINTER DIV. PERSONNEL**

2   Select all the records, including the field names.

3   Define the database.

4   Display the data form.

5   Find the record for Stephen Alexi.

6   Change the spelling of his first name to Steven.

7   Change his salary to $65,529.

8 Enter the following new record.

In this field	Type
Last Name	**Chu**
First Name	**Steven**
Position	**Group Admin. Assist.**
Department	**Marketing**
Salary	**22500**
Start Date	**12/6/88**

9 Prepare the database to be sorted by selecting all the records.

10 Sort the records by department and by ascending order of start date.

The employees who have been employed the longest will be listed first.

Your worksheet should look like this:

	C	D	E	F	G	H
13	Last Name	First Name	Position	Department	Salary	Start Date
14	Hodge	Alex	Unit Mgr.	Admin	$79,148	6/22/79
15	Constance	Burt	Admin. Assist.	Admin	$31,995	5/6/83
16	Price	Ellen	Admin. Assist.	Admin	$29,854	8/1/84
17	Wells	Rose	Cost Accountant	Admin	$38,665	4/15/86
18	McKormick	Brad	Lead Engineer	Engineering	$66,900	12/7/77
19	Silverberg	Jay	Lead Engineer	Engineering	$65,777	10/14/78
20	Alexi	Steven	Lead Engineer	Engineering	$65,529	7/18/80
21	Quan	Karen	Engineering Mgr.	Engineering	$75,462	7/7/83
22	Sofer	Ariel	Senior Engineer	Engineering	$55,765	5/19/84
23	Preston	Liza	Mechanical Engineer	Engineering	$41,525	6/5/84
24	Ferngood	Jules	Senior Engineer	Engineering	$54,332	3/22/85
25	Mann	Alyssa	Mechanical Engineer	Engineering	$37,855	1/20/86
26	Lark	Donald	Software Engineer	Engineering	$41,225	7/12/86
27	Dorfberg	Jeremy	Technician	Engineering	$32,400	2/21/87
28	Cash	Mary	Software Engineer	Engineering	$40,100	9/19/87
29	Plant	Allen	Group Admin. Assist.	Engineering	$23,500	5/23/88
30	Smythe	Leslie	Software Engineer	Engineering	$39,500	10/26/88
31	Petry	Robin	Group Admin. Assist.	Engineering	$22,156	9/6/89
32	Taylor	Ralph	Group Mgr.	Marketing	$74,155	5/7/83
33	Cane	Nate	Product Marketer	Marketing	$56,782	2/3/85
34	Wolf	Hilda	Product Marketer	Marketing	$52,995	3/1/86
35	Seidel	Matt	Product Marketer	Marketing	$47,565	3/30/86

11 Define the database as your print area and print the database.

12 Save and close the worksheet.

Summary and Preview

In this lesson, you learned to:

Define a database on a worksheet   You set up a worksheet database by entering field names, selecting the field names and any data in subsequent rows, and then choosing the Data Set Database command.

Use the data form to add and change database records   You used the Data Form command to enter a new record and change an existing record.

Sort data in a database   You selected records on the worksheet and used the Data Sort command to rearrange their order.

Use the data form to set criteria for selecting database records   You chose the Criteria button and entered comparison criteria in the data form.

Use criteria to find database records   You used criteria in the data form to find and display records.

Delete database records   You used the data form to find and then permanently delete a record from the database.

In the next lesson, you will learn more about using a database. You will set criteria on the worksheet to find, extract, summarize, and analyze database records.

Extracting and Analyzing Data in a Database

You will learn to:

- Set criteria on a worksheet.
- Find records in a database with the Data Find command.
- Find and copy records with the Data Extract command.
- Analyze data with database functions.
- Summarize database records with a data table.

Estimated lesson time: 45 minutes

In this lesson, you will find ways to analyze database records. You will write formulas with database functions and create data tables to quickly summarize your worksheet data.

For more information on worksheet criteria, see Chapter 10, "Analyzing and Reporting Database Information," in the *Microsoft Excel User's Guide*. For more information on database functions, see D*function* in the *Microsoft Excel Function Reference*.

Start the lesson

The LESSON12 worksheet includes personnel records for all three WCS divisions.

1 Open LESSON12.

2 Save the worksheet as **WCS PERSONNEL**

Move the database

When you plan your worksheets, avoid entering data below worksheet databases and extract ranges.

In this lesson, you will add criteria, data analysis, and extract areas to the worksheet. You will make room for these areas by inserting columns and moving the Database Area to the right.

1 Close any other open worksheets.

2 Choose <u>W</u>indow <u>A</u>rrange All.

3 Select cells A17:L78.

Remember, you can use the Formula Goto command to select a range of cells.

4 Choose <u>E</u>dit <u>I</u>nsert.

5 Select the Shift Cells Right option.

6   Choose OK.

When you move a database, you need to redefine it.

7   Select cells O18:U78.

8   Choose <u>D</u>ata Set Data<u>b</u>ase.

Defining a Criteria Range on a Worksheet

In Lesson 11, you set criteria in the data form to find or delete worksheet records. You can also find and delete records by setting criteria on the worksheet. You can use the worksheet criteria range to extract records or analyze records with database functions.

The Data Set Criteria command   You define the criteria range with Data Set Criteria. To set up a criteria range, copy the database field names to another area of the worksheet. Select the field names along with the cells in the next row and choose the Data Set Criteria command. Microsoft Excel names your selection "Criteria."

Define the criteria range

Reduce the possibility of typing errors by copying field names to the criteria range.

You will define a criteria range for finding and extracting records from the worksheet database. Start by copying the field names to the criteria range. Then select the field names and the row beneath and choose Data Set Criteria.

1   Select cells O18:U18, the database field names.

2   Choose <u>E</u>dit <u>C</u>opy.

3   Select cell C18.

4   Choose <u>E</u>dit <u>P</u>aste.

5   Select cells C18:I19.

6   Choose <u>D</u>ata Set <u>C</u>riteria.

You have defined the criteria range. Now you will label the area.

Label the criteria area

1   In cell A17, type **Criteria Area**

2   Click the enter box or press ENTER.

3   From the style list on the tool bar, select the Title style.

4   Choose Forma<u>t</u> <u>A</u>lignment.

5   Under Alignment, select the Right option.

6   Turn on the Wrap Text check box.

7   Choose OK.

Your worksheet should look like this:

	A	B	C	D	E	F	G	H
17	Criteria Area							
18			Last Name	First Name	Position	Department	Division	Salary
19								
20								

Enter criteria

Now you will enter criteria in the worksheet to find all employees in the Engineering Department who earn $40,000 or more per year.

1 Select cell F19, the Department criterion cell.

2 Type **Engineering**

3 Click the enter box or press ENTER.

4 Select cell H19, the Salary criterion cell.

5 Type **>=40000**

6 Click the enter box or press ENTER.

The Criteria Area of your worksheet should look like this:

	A	B	C	D	E	F	G	H	
17	Criteria Area								
18			Last Name	First Name	Position	Department	Division	Salary	Sta
19						Engineering		>=40000	

You defined the criteria range with the Data Set Criteria command before you entered the criteria. You can change the criteria in the cells once the criteria range has been defined.

Finding Worksheet Database Records

View individual records that match your criteria with the Data Find command.

The Data Find command   With Data Find, you can select records in the database range that match the criteria in the criteria range. Press the UP ARROW or DOWN ARROW key or click the scroll arrow to select the matching records. To cancel Find mode, choose Data Exit Find or press COMMAND+PERIOD or ESC.

The Data Delete command   With Data Delete, you can delete from the database all records that match the criteria in the criteria range. You should test your criteria with the Data Find command before you delete records, because you cannot undo Data Delete.

Find the records that match the criteria

Now you will use the Data Find command to find the records that match your criteria: employees in the Engineering Department who earn $40,000 or more each year.

1 Choose Data Find.

   📁   Press COMMAND+F.

Microsoft Excel finds the first record that meets these criteria. Your worksheet should look like this:

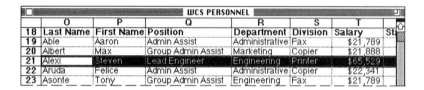

	O	P	Q	R	S	T	St
18	Last Name	First Name	Position	Department	Division	Salary	
19	Able	Aaron	Admin Assist	Administrative	Fax	$21,789	
20	Albert	Max	Group Admin Assist	Marketing	Copier	$21,888	
21	Alexi	Steven	Lead Engineer	Engineering	Printer	$65,529	
22	Aruda	Felice	Admin Assist	Administrative	Copier	$22,341	
23	Asonte	Tony	Group Admin Assist	Engineering	Fax	$21,789	

2 Click the down scroll arrow to view the remaining matching records.

   📁   Press the ARROW keys.

3 Choose Data Exit Find to end the search for records matching your criteria.

   📁   Press COMMAND+PERIOD or ESC.

Wildcard criteria   You can use the *wildcard characters*, asterisk (*) and question mark (?), to establish criteria for finding and extracting data. Substitute the asterisk (*) when you want to find a string that is a subset of a larger string. For example, typing ***mgr** as the criterion for the Position field will find the records of employees with titles such as Group Marketing Mgr., Engineering Mgr., and so on. Substitute the question mark (?) for a single character in a text string. For example, if you type **Sm?th** in the Last Name field, Microsoft Excel will find the name Smith or Smyth.

Set criteria to match the records of all engineers

You will change the criteria to find the records of all engineers in the worksheet database. First, clear the existing criteria from the criteria range.

1 Select cells F19:H19.

2 Choose Edit Clear.

3 Choose OK.

4 Select cell E19, the Position criterion.

5 Type ***Engineer**

6 Click the enter box or press ENTER.

The Criteria Area on your worksheet should look like this:

	C	D	E	F	G	H	I
17							
18	Last Name	First Name	Position	Department	Division	Salary	Start Date
19			*Engineer				
20							

Extracting Worksheet Database Records

You can find and copy records from a worksheet database to another cell range called an *extract* range.

Use Data Extract to extract records to create a report.

The Data Extract command   With Data Extract, you can copy the database records that match your criteria into a separate extract range. You can do this in two ways. You can copy the database field names to your extract range, select the field names, and choose Data Extract. Or you can define the extract range in advance with the Data Set Extract command.

The Data Set Extract command   If you use Data Set Extract to define the extract range, you don't need to select the extract range every time you extract data. Select the extract range and choose Data Set Extract. Then you can choose Data Extract when you are ready. This command is especially useful if you need to extract data while you are working in another part of a large database.

Extract the records for all engineers

You can use any combination of field names in the extract range.

You'll use the criteria set in the previous procedure to find and copy, or extract, all the records of West Coast Sales engineers. First you will copy the first five field names from the database to the extract range. Don't include the Salary or Start Date field names.

1 Select cells C18:G18.

2 Choose Edit Copy.

3 Select cell C23.

4 Choose Edit Paste.

The pasted field names should still be selected.

5 Choose Data Extract.

✍ Press COMMAND+E.

6 Turn on the Unique Records Only check box.

Microsoft Excel will extract only the first of duplicate records.

7 Choose OK.

Only the data for the fields that you selected is extracted. The Data Extract command finds all records that match the criteria and copies them to the extract range. Your worksheet should look like this:

	A	B	C	D	E	F	G
17	**Criteria Area**						
18			Last Name	First Name	Position	Department	Division
19					*Engineer		
20							
21							
22							
23			Last Name	First Name	Position	Department	Division
24			Alexi	Steven	Lead Engineer	Engineering	Printer
25			Beech	Susan	Senior Engineer	Engineering	Copier
26			Berg	Bobby	Engineering Mgr.	Engineering	Fax
27			Cash	Mary	Software Engineer	Engineering	Printer
28			Coyne	Dennis	Software Engineer	Engineering	Copier
29			Ferngood	Jules	Senior Engineer	Engineering	Printer
30			Fine	Caroline	Engineering Mgr.	Engineering	Copier
31			Johnson	Miguel	Senior Engineer	Engineering	Copier
32			Lark	Donald	Software Engineer	Engineering	Printer
33			Lin	Michael	Software Engineer	Engineering	Fax
34			Mann	Alyssa	Mechanical Engineer	Engineering	Printer
35			McKormick	Brad	Lead Engineer	Engineering	Printer
36			North	Roberta	Mechanical Engineer	Engineering	Fax
37			Preston	Liza	Mechanical Engineer	Engineering	Printer
38			Quan	Karen	Engineering Mgr.	Engineering	Printer
39			Silverberg	Jay	Lead Engineer	Engineering	Printer
40			Smythe	Leslie	Software Engineer	Engineering	Printer
41			Sofer	Ariel	Senior Engineer	Engineering	Printer
42			Weston	Sam	Senior Engineer	Engineering	Fax
43			White	Jessica	Mechanical Engineer	Engineering	Copier
44							

Data below the extract range will be deleted.

Rather than selecting only the field names for the extract range, you can select enough rows to accommodate all the extracted records. Only the cells within the selection are cleared before the records are copied. When you select only the field names, all subsequent rows below the field names are cleared before the records are copied.

Combining criteria   You can also combine criteria. You already used two criteria in a criteria range to select all members of the Engineering Department who earn more than $40,000. If you add a second row to your criteria range, Microsoft Excel finds records that match the criteria in the first row or the second row. You can also combine criteria by entering a field name twice in the criteria range and specifying two criteria for the same field.

Extract records that meet either criterion

A meeting is scheduled for all administrative personnel in the Copier Division. The meeting will include all members of the Administrative Department, but only the group administrative assistants from the other departments within the Copier Division. You need to set up criteria to find employees who are members of the Administrative Department, or whose job title is "Group Admin. Assist."

1 Select cell E19.

2 Choose Edit Clear.

3 Choose OK.

4 Select cells C18:I20.

5 Choose Data Set Criteria.

6 In the Criteria Area, type the following:

	A	B	C	D	E	F	G
17	**Criteria Area**						
18			Last Name	First Name	Position	Department	Division
19						Admin	Copier
20					*Admin		Copier
21							

The criteria will find employees of the Copier Division who belong to the Administrative Department, or whose title includes "Admin."

Set the extract range and extract the records

1 Select cells C23:G23.

2 Choose Data Set Extract.

3 Choose Data Extract.

  ✒ Press COMMAND+E.

4 Choose OK.

Your worksheet should look like this:

	C	D	E	F	G
23	Last Name	First Name	Position	Department	Division
24	Albert	Max	Group Admin.Assist.	Marketing	Copier
25	Aruda	Felice	Admin.Assist.	Admin	Copier
26	Davison	Karen	Unit Mgr.	Admin	Copier
27	Raye	Alice	Group Admin.Assist	Engineering	Copier
28	Richards	Phillip	Cost Accountant	Admin	Copier
29	Wells	Jason	Admin.Assist.	Admin	Copier
30					

Label the extract area

1 Select cell A22.

2 Type **Extract Area**

3 Click the enter box or press ENTER.

4 From the style list on the tool bar, select the Title style.

5 Using the Format Alignment command, format cell A22 to look like cell A17.

Analyzing Data

Using database functions to summarize information   With database functions such as DSUM, DCOUNT, and DAVERAGE, you can summarize worksheet data from a database. You can use the Formula Paste Function command to paste a database function into a cell.

The arguments for each database function are the same (*database, field, criteria*). The *database* argument can be the name Database, another named range, or a reference to a range. The *field* argument can be the field name in quotation marks, the field number, or the cell reference of the field name. The *criteria* argument can be the name Criteria, another named range, or a reference to a range.

Insert rows for an analysis area

Before you analyze the database, you will insert a Data Analysis Area. You will insert a range of cells rather than entire rows to avoid inserting rows between the records in the Database Area, which is out of sight to the right of the Criteria and Extract Areas.

1 Select cells A22:G40.

2 Choose Edit Insert.

3 Select the Shift Cells Down option.

4 Choose OK.

5 Scroll to the right until you can see the database.

You inserted cells to move the Extract Area down but did not affect the database.

Use the DSUM function in a formula

You can create a formula that sums the salaries for the employees who meet the criteria.

1 In cells A23 and C25, type and format the labels as shown in the following illustration:

	A	B	C	D
23	**Data Analysis Area**			
24				
25			Admin Salaries	
26				

2 Select cell D25.

3 Choose Formula Paste Function.

4 Select the DSUM( ) function.

5 Choose OK.

6 Select the *field* argument in the formula bar.

7 Type **"Salary"**

Make sure to type the quotation marks around "Salary".

8 Click the enter box or press ENTER.

9 In the style list on the tool bar, select the Currency 0 Decimals style.

The total of administrative salaries, $209,919, appears in cell D25.

Change the criterion and calculate all engineer salaries

Now change the criterion and total the salaries for all engineers.

1 Select cell C25.

2 Type **Engineer Salaries**

3 Click the enter box or press ENTER.

You can use the Format Column Width command to widen the column.

4 Select cells E19:G20.

5 Choose Edit Clear to clear the criteria from these cells.

6 Choose OK.

7 Select cell E19.

8 Type ***Engineer**

9 Click the enter box or press ENTER.

10 Select cells C18:I19.

11 Choose <u>D</u>ata Set <u>C</u>riteria.

You need to redefine the criteria so as not to include a blank row, which would calculate all salaries.

The total of salaries for the Engineering Departments in all three divisions, $1,051,305, appears in cell D25.

The Data Table command You can use the Data Table command to analyze your worksheet database with several criteria at once. A *data table* is a range of cells that shows the results of substituting different values in one or more formulas. It can be most useful when you want to summarize a field of data according to different criteria. For example, you might want to compare the salaries for similar positions in different departments or divisions in the company.

Summarize department salaries by division

You will use a data table to summarize and compare the salaries by division for each department. The Data Table command will calculate the salaries for each department within each division and display the results in the table.

1 Clear cell E19.

2 Type the following labels in cells C25, D26:D29, and E25:G25:

	C	D	E	F	G
25	Total Salaries	$2,727,206	Copier	Fax	Printer
26		Admin			
27		Engineering			
28		Marketing			
29		R and D			
30					

3 Select cells D25:G29.

4 Choose <u>D</u>ata <u>T</u>able.

    ▢ To get Help on the Data Table command, press COMMAND+SHIFT+ QUESTION MARK while the Data Table dialog box is displayed.

5 To enter the Row Input Cell, select cell G19 or type **g19**

You can move the dialog box if it's in your way.

6 To enter the Column Input Cell, select cell F19 or type **f19**

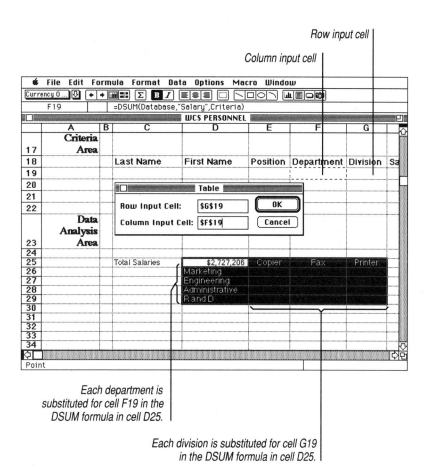

Row input cell

Column input cell

Each department is substituted for cell F19 in the DSUM formula in cell D25.

Each division is substituted for cell G19 in the DSUM formula in cell D25.

7   Choose OK.

8   Select cells E26:G29.

9   In the style list on the tool bar, select the Currency 0 Decimals style.

10   If necessary, use the Format Column Width command to see all your data.

The salaries for each department within the three divisions appear in the data table. Your worksheet should look like this:

	C	D	E	F	G
25	Total Salaries	$2,727,206	Copier	Fax	Printer
26		Admin	$164,033	$133,694	$179,662
27		Engineering	$312,556	$255,564	$662,026
28		Marketing	$178,718	$106,313	$322,198
29		R and D	$99,208	$98,116	$215,118
30					

Save the worksheet

You will continue to use the WCS PERSONNEL worksheet in the "You Try It" exercise.

▶ Choose File Save to save WCS PERSONNEL.

You Try It

In the preceding procedure, you found the total salaries for each department in each division. Now you will create a data table to compare the number of employees for each department within each division. You will continue to use the WCS PERSONNEL worksheet for this exercise.

You will copy the table you created to another cell range in the Data Analysis Area, clear the previous results, replace the DSUM function with the DCOUNTA function to count the number of nonblank cells, and replace "Salary" with "Last Name" for the field argument. Then, you will choose the Data Table command and enter the reference of the division criterion in the Row Input Cell and the reference of the department criterion in the Column Input Cell. The Data Table command will calculate the number of employees for each department within its respective divisions and display the results in the table.

1 Copy the Salary table and paste it into cells C33:G37.

2 Clear the data in cells E34:G37.

3 Use the style box on the tool bar to apply the Normal style to cells D33 and E34:G37.

4 In cell C33, change Total Salaries to Total Employees.

   Use the Format Column Width command, if necessary, to display the text.

5 Paste the DCOUNTA function into cell D33.

6 Replace the *field* argument with **"Last Name"**

7 Select cells D33:G37.

8 Choose Data Table.

9 In the Row Input Cell box, enter **g19**, the cell for the Division criterion.

10 In the Column Input Cell box, enter **f19**, the cell for the Department criterion.

11 Choose OK.

   This table counts the number of employees in each department within each division.

12 Format the worksheet by adding titles, text formatting, and borders. Use the completed worksheet shown in the following illustration as an example.

	A	B	C	D	E	F	G	H
22								
23	Data Analysis Area			Comparison of Divisions by Department				
24								
25			Total Salaries	$2,727,206	Copier	Fax	Printer	
26				Admin.	$164,033	$133,694	$179,662	
27				Engineering	$312,556	$255,564	$662,026	
28				Marketing	$178,718	$106,313	$322,198	
29				R and D	$99,208	$98,116	$215,118	
30								
31								
32								
33			Total Employees	60	Copier	Fax	Printer	
34				Admin.	4	3	4	
35				Engineering	7	6	14	
36				Marketing	4	2	7	
37				R and D	2	2	5	
38								
39								

13 Print the Data Analysis Area.

14 Save and close the worksheet when you are finished.

Summary and Preview

In this lesson, you learned to:

Set criteria on a worksheet   You set worksheet criteria by copying field names from the worksheet database to another cell range, selecting the pasted field names and the following row, and choosing the Data Set Criteria command.

Find records in a database with the Data Find command   You used the Data Find command to view records that match worksheet criteria.

Find and copy records with the Data Extract command   You used the Data Extract command to find records that match worksheet criteria and copy them to an extract range.

Analyze data with database functions   You used database functions to summarize fields of data that match worksheet criteria within a database.

Summarize database records with a data table   You created a data table that uses a database function to summarize a field of data matching multiple criteria.

In the next lesson, you will learn to display information graphically. You will learn to create charts as separate documents or embedded on your worksheet for reports and presentations.

5 Creating Charts

Creating a Chart

You will learn to:

- Select worksheet data to create a new chart.
- Embed a chart in a worksheet.
- Create a separate chart document.
- Change the chart type.
- Add a chart legend.
- Add a title to a chart.
- Add chart gridlines.

Estimated lesson time: 25 minutes

A chart displays worksheet data graphically.

In this lesson, you will learn how to display worksheet data in a chart that is either embedded in your worksheet or in a separate document. You will choose the chart type that best presents your data, add text for the chart title, and label the chart axes.

For more information on creating a chart, see Chapter 11, "Creating a Chart," in the *Microsoft Excel User's Guide*.

Start the lesson

You will plot a chart from data in the SALES HISTORY worksheet. Open the LESSON13 worksheet and rename it SALES HISTORY.

1 Open the LESSON13 worksheet.

2 Save the worksheet as **SALES HISTORY**

Selecting Worksheet Data

Select the worksheet data for the chart

As with other Microsoft Excel commands, the items you select before you choose the command determine what the command does.

Your chart will compare annual sales for the company and the entire industry from 1982 to 1991. Select the worksheet data to include in the chart, omitting the 1992 data for now.

1 Close any other open worksheets.

2 If necessary, choose <u>W</u>indow <u>A</u>rrange All.

3 Select cells C9:E19.

Your worksheet should look like this:

```
 File  Edit  Formula  Format  Data  Options  Macro  Window

Normal
         C9
                            SALES HISTORY
        A        B    C       D        E        F      G      H
 1          Title      WCS Ten Year Sales History
 2        Created by   Sam Bryan
 3      Date Modified  17-Jun-91
 4
 5         Purpose     This worksheet summarizes West Coast Sales' gross
 6                     revenue for the previous ten years.
 7
 8      Sales History
 9                     Year   Company  Industry
10                     1982    $62,947  $1,210,000
11                     1983    $69,941  $1,230,000
12                     1984    $93,254  $1,260,000
13                     1985   $124,339  $1,300,000
14                     1986   $138,155  $1,350,000
15                     1987   $162,535  $1,380,000
16                     1988   $205,740  $1,370,000
17                     1989   $233,796  $1,400,000
18                     1990   $320,268  $1,500,000
19                     1991   $363,941  $1,690,000
20                     1992   $424,491  $2,000,000
21
22
Ready
```

Creating a New Chart

You can embed a chart in your worksheet with the chart tool or create a chart document with the File New command.

To create a new chart, you first select the worksheet data you want to display in the chart, and then create a new chart with either the chart tool or the File New command. Microsoft Excel classifies the data in your worksheet selection in a way that makes sense for the chart.

The chart tool   You can use the chart tool to embed a chart in your worksheet. Charts created with the chart tool are graphic objects that are saved and printed with the worksheet and always reflect the latest worksheet data. You must have a mouse to use the chart tool.

Chart tool

The File New command   You can use the File New command to create a chart as a separate document. Use the File New command to create a chart if you want to open and print a chart separately, if you want several worksheets to supply source data to the chart, or if you don't want the chart taking up space on the worksheet.

Data series and categories   When you create a new chart, Microsoft Excel classifies your selected worksheet data into data series and categories.

In general, Microsoft Excel defines data series and categories according to the number of rows and columns in your worksheet selection. Unless you specify otherwise, Microsoft Excel assumes you want fewer data series than categories.

In this case, Microsoft Excel will define the data in column D as the "Company" data series and the data in column E as the "Industry" data series. The selected years in column C will be categories.

Create a chart with the chart tool

With your worksheet data selected, use the chart tool to embed a chart in the worksheet.

1   Click the chart tool (📊).

The mouse pointer turns into a cross hair.

2   Position the pointer at cell A22.

3   Hold down COMMAND and drag the dotted box to cell F34.

Pressing COMMAND aligns the chart with the worksheet grid.

When you release the mouse button, Microsoft Excel displays a chart in the default chart format. Your worksheet should look like this:

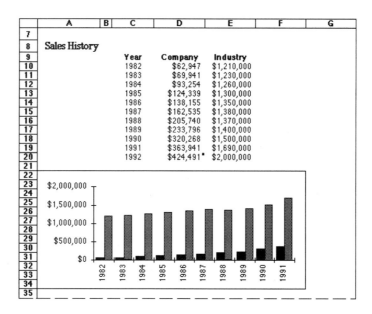

If you decide you want to work with this chart in a separate document, you can save it as a separate document or use the File New command to create a new chart document with the same data. Consider the type of formatting the chart will require. In addition to the formatting available on separate charts—attached and unattached text, legends, and arrows—an embedded chart can use objects available on worksheets, such as text boxes. You will create a worksheet presentation using worksheet objects and embedded charts in Lesson 16, "Using Embedded Charts and Worksheet Graphics."

Create and save a new chart document

With the same worksheet data selected, use the File New command to create a new chart document. Name and save the chart with the File Save As command. Enlarge the chart window so you have more room to work on the chart.

1 Select cells C9:E19 again and choose File New.

2 Select Chart.

3 Choose OK.

4 Choose File Save As.

5 In the Save Chart As box, type **SALES CHART**

6 Choose the Save button.

   The chart name appears in the title bar of the chart window.

7 In the upper-right corner of the SALES CHART window, click the zoom box.

Your chart window should look like this:

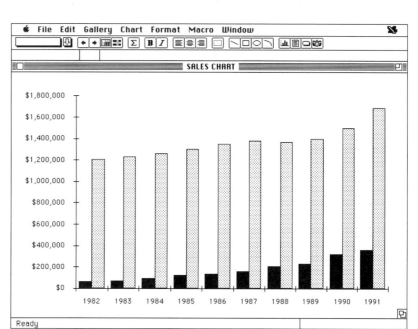

In Microsoft Excel, you can see the chart while you're working on it.

The chart window   The entire chart window is the *chart area*. The rectangle defined by the two axes is the *plot area*. On your chart, the vertical (y) axis is the value axis; it displays dollar values. The horizontal (x) axis is the category axis; it displays years as category names.

Choosing a Chart Type from the Gallery

Microsoft Excel displays a column chart by default, but you can change the chart type by choosing a command from the Gallery menu.

Microsoft Excel has 68 built-in chart formats.

Microsoft Excel has seven two-dimensional chart types and four three-dimensional (3-D) chart types. The two-dimensional chart types are area, bar, column, line, pie, xy (scatter), and combination. The three-dimensional chart types are 3-D area, 3-D column, 3-D line, and 3-D pie. When you choose a chart type from the Gallery menu, a gallery appears showing the available variations for that chart type.

Scroll through the galleries

If you're not sure which chart type you want, you can scroll from one gallery to another without choosing a command.

1 Choose Gallery Area.

> ☑ To get Help on the Gallery Area command, press COMMAND+SHIFT+ QUESTION MARK while the Gallery Area dialog box is displayed.

2 Choose the Next button.

The bar chart gallery is displayed.

3 Continue choosing the Next button until the combination chart gallery is displayed.

Change to a combination chart

You can create a chart that combines two chart types.

You can use a combination of two chart types to compare the trends in your data.

1 With the combination chart gallery still displayed, select combination chart format 2.

2 Choose OK.

Your chart should look like this:

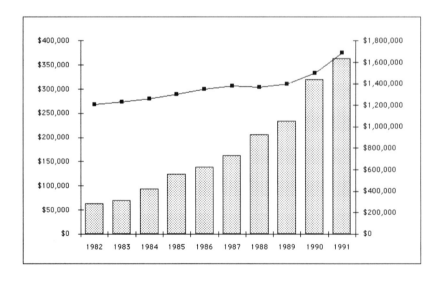

The combination chart has two value axes so you can compare trends. The left value axis is for the columns that show company sales. The right value axis is for the line that shows industry sales.

Pie charts and xy charts   A pie chart is used when you have only one data series. An xy (scatter) chart is used to plot values when you expect to see a relationship between values in one data series and values in another data series. An xy chart has no categories. You'll create an xy chart in Lesson 15, "Editing Chart Data Series."

3-D charts   Use three-dimensional (3-D) charts to show relationships between two categories of information and one set of values. A 3-D chart has an additional axis. The z axis is the horizontal value axis, the category labels are plotted along the x axis, and the series names are plotted along the y axis. You will create a 3-D column chart in the "You Try It" exercise at the end of this lesson.

Adding a Legend

The legend identifies each data series.

When you add a legend to your chart, Microsoft Excel automatically uses your data series names for the legend.

Add a chart legend

By default, the legend appears to the right of the plot area. You'll learn how to move the legend in Lesson 14, "Formatting a Chart."

▶ Choose Chart Add Legend.

Your chart should look like this:

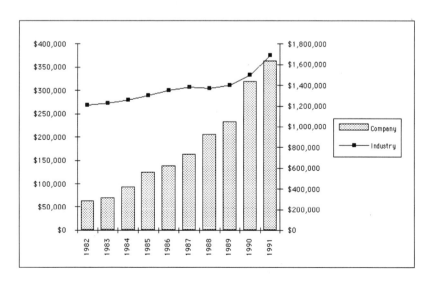

The Chart Delete Legend command You can have only one chart legend. After you add a legend, the Chart Add Legend command becomes the Chart Delete Legend command. When you choose Chart Delete Legend to remove the legend, the Chart Add Legend command appears in the menu again.

Adding Text

When you add text as a chart title or axis title, the text is attached to a specific part of the chart and can't be moved. You'll learn how to add unattached text to a chart in Lesson 14, "Formatting a Chart."

Use Chart Attach Text to add a title to the chart or a label to an axis.

The Chart Attach Text command With Chart Attach Text, you can attach text to a certain part of a chart, such as an axis and data points. After you add the text, you can edit it in the formula bar.

Attach a title to the chart

1 Choose Chart Attach Text.

Chart Title is already selected.

2 Choose OK.

"Title" appears at the top of the chart.

3 Type **Company vs. Industry-Wide Sales**

Your title appears in the formula bar as you type.

4 Click the enter box or press ENTER.

Your chart should look like this:

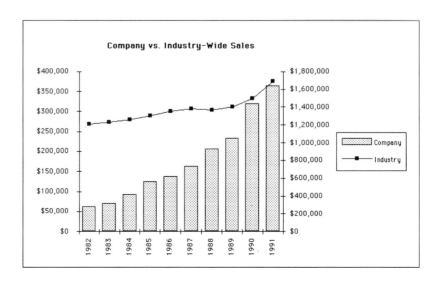

Label the y axis

1 Choose Chart Attach Text.
2 Under Attach Text To, select the Value (Y) Axis option.
3 Choose OK.

"Y" appears along the y axis of the chart.

4 Type **Company**
5 Click the enter box or press ENTER.

Label the x axis

1 Choose Chart Attach Text.
2 Under Attach Text To, select the Category (X) Axis option.
3 Choose OK.

"X" appears along the x axis of the chart.

4 Type **Year**
5 Click the enter box or press ENTER.

Your chart should look like this:

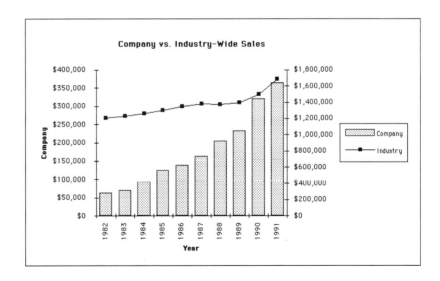

Adding Gridlines

The Chart Gridlines command With Chart Gridlines, you can control the display of major and minor gridlines for both axes.

Add major gridlines to the y axis

1 Choose Chart Gridlines.

2 Under Value (Y) Axis, turn on the Major Gridlines check box.

3 Choose OK.

Your chart should look like this:

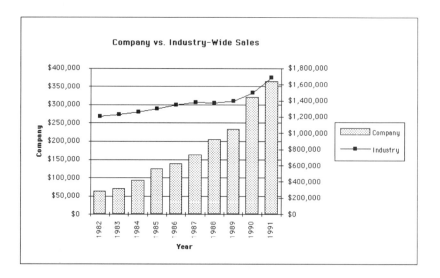

Save your work

Save the SALES HISTORY worksheet and the SALES CHART document as a workspace file. You'll continue working on the SALES CHART document in the next lesson.

1 Choose File Save Workspace.

2 In the Save Workspace As box, type **LESSON13 WORKSPACE**

3 Choose the Save button.

4 Choose the Yes button to save the changes in SALES HISTORY.

5 Choose the Yes button to save the changes in SALES CHART.

Close the documents

▶ Choose File Close All to close the worksheet and chart.

You Try It

In this exercise, you will create two charts from data tables summarizing database records. You created the tables in the previous lesson to compare the number of personnel and total of salaries for each department within the Fax, Copier, and Printer Divisions of West Coast Sales. You will create a 3-D column chart for each table. To change the size of the chart, resize the chart window.

1   Open the UTRYIT13 worksheet.

2   Select cells D25:G29.

3   Use the File New command to create a chart document.

4   Save the chart with the name **SALARY CHART**

5   Change the chart type to a 3-D column chart with gridlines (format 6).

6   Add a legend to the chart.

7   Add the chart title **Departmental Salaries**

8   On the UTRYIT13 worksheet, select cells D33:G37.

9   Repeat steps 3 through 7, saving the chart document as **EMPLOYEE CHART** and titling the chart **Number of Departmental Employees**

You can compare the SALARY13 CHART and EMPLOYEE13 CHART documents with your results. Save and close all the documents when you are finished.

Summary and Preview

In this lesson, you learned to:

Select worksheet data to create a new chart   You selected a range of cells including information you want to chart.

Embed a chart in a worksheet   You created an embedded chart in the worksheet by clicking the chart tool and dragging the mouse pointer across the worksheet.

Create a separate chart document   You used the File New command to create a new chart in a separate document.

Change the chart type   You explored the chart types to find an appropriate chart type for your data.

Add a chart legend   You used the Chart Add Legend command to add a legend to your chart.

Add a title to the chart You used the Chart Attach Text command to add a title to the chart and label the axes.

Add chart gridlines You used the Chart Gridlines command to add gridlines to your chart.

In the next lesson, you'll learn how to select and move objects in your chart. You'll format your chart to improve its appearance and make it easier to understand.

Formatting a Chart

You will learn to:

- Select chart objects with the mouse or keyboard.
- Change fonts and patterns of chart objects.
- Move and size chart objects.
- Add an arrow to a chart.
- Add unattached text to a chart.
- Save a chart as a template.

Estimated lesson time: 30 minutes

In this lesson, you will format your SALES CHART document. You will learn how to select chart objects so you can move and format them. You will change the font and pattern of objects and add new objects to the chart.

You'll also save your customized chart formatting in a template file, which you can use to create similar charts.

For more information on formatting a chart, see Chapter 13, "Formatting a Chart," in the *Microsoft Excel User's Guide*.

Start the lesson

Open the LESSON14 WORKSPACE file. This workspace file includes the LESSON14 worksheet and the LESSON14 CHART. Rename the worksheet SALES HISTORY and the chart SALES CHART.

1 Open LESSON14 WORKSPACE.

2 Switch to the LESSON14 worksheet.

3 Rename the worksheet **SALES HISTORY**

4 If you are asked if you want to replace the existing document, choose the Yes button.

5 Switch to LESSON14 CHART.

6 Rename the chart **SALES CHART**

7 If you are asked whether you want to replace the existing document, choose the Yes button.

8 Click the zoom box to expand the chart window.

Selecting Chart Objects

Select chart objects with the mouse or keyboard before you format them.

You select the chart objects you want to act on before you choose a command, just as you select the worksheet cells you want to act on before choosing a command. You can select chart objects with the mouse or the keyboard. A selected chart object is surrounded with white or black selection squares. Black selection squares are handles you can drag to move the object. White selection squares mean the object can't be moved.

Selecting a chart object with the mouse   To select a chart object with the mouse, click the object.

Selecting a chart object with the keyboard   To select a chart object with the keyboard, use the ARROW keys. You can press the LEFT ARROW or RIGHT ARROW key to move to any individual object. You can also press the UP ARROW or DOWN ARROW key to move between classes of objects, and then press the LEFT ARROW or RIGHT ARROW key to move to the individual object you want. Microsoft Excel groups chart objects into the following classes:

- Chart area
- Plot area
- Legend
- Axes
- Chart text

- Chart arrows
- Gridlines
- First data series
- Second data series, and so on

Moving and Formatting the Legend

You can move the chart legend with the Format Legend command or by dragging it with the mouse.

The Format Legend command   You can position a legend in one of four places on a chart with the Format Legend command. The horizontal or vertical orientation of the legend depends on its position. In the Format Legend dialog box, you can choose the Patterns or Font button to open another dialog box and format the legend.

Moving the legend with the mouse   You can move a legend on the chart by dragging it with the mouse. If you drag the legend to the left or right side of the chart, it will be oriented vertically. If you drag the legend above or below the chart, it will be oriented horizontally.

Move the legend

▶ Drag the chart legend to the bottom of the chart.

　✍ Press the DOWN ARROW key until the legend is selected. Choose the Forma̲t L̲egend command. Under Type, select the Bottom option. Don't choose OK yet.

If you use the Format Legend command to move the legend, you can also choose the Font button or the Patterns button to make additional changes to the legend.

Choosing buttons to bypass the Format menu   You can move directly from one Format dialog box to another by choosing buttons in the dialog box. You can save time by choosing a button instead of choosing another command from the menu.

Change the legend pattern

Remove the legend border and change the legend color.

You can also double-click the legend to open the Format Patterns dialog box.

1   If you moved the legend with the mouse, choose Format Patterns.

   If you moved the legend with the Format Legend command, choose the Patterns button.

   ▣   To get Help on the Format Patterns command, press COMMAND+ SHIFT+QUESTION MARK while the Format Patterns dialog box is displayed.

2   Under Border, select the None option.

3   Under Area, select the third pattern from the Pattern list.

   Don't choose OK yet.

Change the legend font

You can save time by choosing the Font button, instead of closing the dialog box and then choosing the Format Font command. You'll change the font, size, and color of the text in the legend.

1   Choose the Font button.

2   In the Font box, select Times.

3   In the Size box, select 12.

4   Under Style, turn on the Bold check box.

5   In the Color list, select blue.

6   Choose OK.

Your chart should look like this:

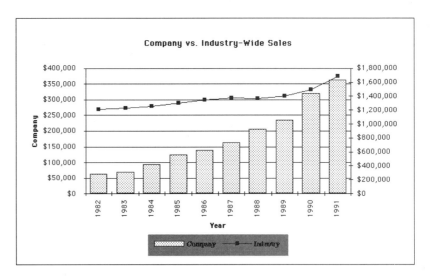

Formatting the Chart Area

The Chart Select Chart command   You can use the mouse, the ARROW keys, or the Chart Select Chart command to select the chart area. You select the chart area when you want to change fonts or patterns for the chart, clear formats with the Edit Clear command, or copy chart attributes to another chart with Edit Copy.

Apply a shadow border and different pattern to the chart area

You'll create a shadow border around the entire chart and change the color of the chart to match that of the legend.

1 Choose Chart Select Chart.

2 Choose Format Patterns.

3 In the Weight list, select the third line weight.

4 Under Border, turn on the Shadow check box.

5 Under Area, select the third pattern from the Pattern list.

6 Choose OK.

Your chart should look like this:

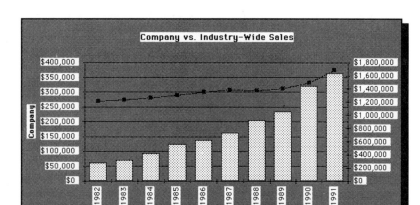

Formatting the Plot Area

The Chart Select Plot Area command   You can use the mouse, the ARROW keys, or the Chart Select Plot Area command to select the plot area. You select the plot area before formatting it with the Format Patterns command.

Change the color of the plot area

You'll change the color of the plot area to make the plotted data stand out from the rest of the chart.

1   Choose Chart Select Plot Area.

2   Choose Format Patterns.

3   Under Area, select white from the Foreground list.

4   Choose OK.

Your chart should look like this:

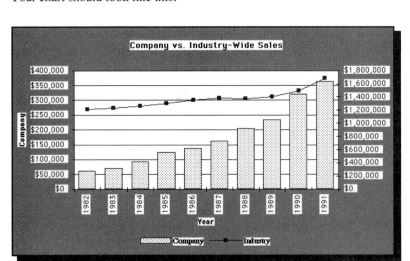

Formatting the Text

Change the font of the y-axis label

You'll use the Format Font command to change the font and color of the y-axis label.

1 Select the y-axis label, "Company."

2 Choose Format Font.

3 In the Font box, select Times.

4 In the Size box, select 12.

5 In the Color list, select blue.

6 Choose OK.

Repeat the format for the x-axis label

You can use the Edit Repeat Font command to repeat your formatting for the x-axis label.

1 Select the x-axis label, "Year."

2 Choose Edit Repeat Font.

Your chart should look like this:

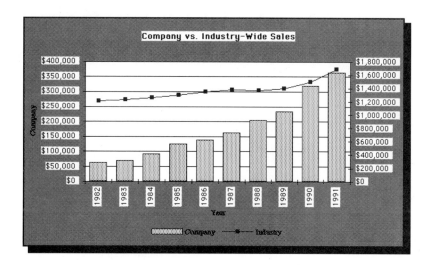

Change the font and pattern of the chart title

You can use the Edit Repeat Font command again to repeat your formatting changes for the chart title. Use the Format Font command to increase the font size to 14 points. Then choose the Patterns button to add a border around the chart title and change its color.

1 Select the chart title, "Company vs. Industry-Wide Sales."

2 Choose Edit Repeat Font.

3 Choose Format Font.

4 In the Size box, select 14.

5 Choose the Patterns button.

6 Under Border, turn on the Shadow check box.

7 Under Area, select white from the Foreground list.

8 Choose OK.

Your chart should look like this:

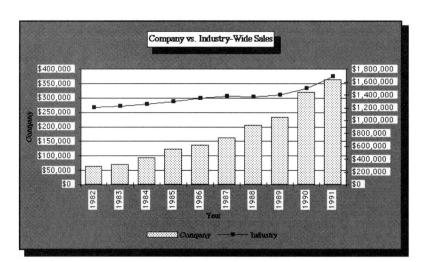

Save your work

▶ Choose File Save.

Saving the Chart as a Template

You can save your chart settings and formatting in a chart template so that you can create other charts later without going through all the formatting steps.

Templates in the Excel Startup folder are listed in the File New dialog box.

Saving a chart template   You save a chart as a template with the File Save As command. If you save a template in the Excel Startup folder, it will appear in the File New dialog box in your next Microsoft Excel session.

Save a chart template

You will use SALES CHART as a template to create other charts in later lessons.

1 Choose File Save As.

2 Name the template **SALES CHART TEMPLATE**

3 Choose the Options button.

4 In the File Format list, select Template.

5 Choose OK to save the format.

6 Choose the Save button.

Now you'll be able to reuse your chart settings and formatting by opening the SALES CHART TEMPLATE.

Close the template and reopen the chart

You will use the formatting currently in the template for other worksheets in later lessons. Close the template and reopen the original chart document to continue your work.

1 Close the template document.

2 Reopen SALES CHART.

If you have a large-screen Macintosh, you can choose the filename from the recently opened file list at the bottom of the File menu.

Adding an Arrow

You can use arrows to point to important chart information.

You can add one or more arrows to a chart to point out important information. You can move, size, and format the arrows to give them the appearance you want.

The Chart Add Arrow command   Chart Add Arrow adds an arrow to the active chart window.

The Chart Delete Arrow command   Chart Delete Arrow deletes the selected arrow from a chart.

You'll add an arrow to your chart to highlight gains in the company's percentage of market share.

Add an arrow

▶ Choose Chart Add Arrow.

You need to move, size, and format the arrow.

Moving and sizing an arrow with the mouse   To change the orientation and length of an arrow, drag either of its end points. You can rotate the arrow and change its length in one step. To move the entire arrow, drag the shaft.

Moving and sizing an arrow with the keyboard   To size an arrow, select it and choose the Format Size command. Use the ARROW keys to change the orientation and length, and then press ENTER. To move the entire arrow, select it and choose the Format Move command. Use the ARROW keys to position the arrow, and then press ENTER.

Size the arrow

Shorten the arrow and rotate it so it points to the left.

▶ Drag the arrow point up and left.

You still need to move the arrow.

Move the arrow

Move the arrow so it points to the 1991 sales data.

▶ Drag the arrow to the right by the shaft.

Format the arrow

You will use the Format Patterns command to change the color and weight of the arrow.

You can open the Format Patterns dialog box by double-clicking a chart object.

1 Double-click the arrow to open the Format Patterns dialog box.

2 Under Line, select the second line weight in the Weight list.

3 In the Color list, select blue.

4 Choose OK.

Your chart should look like this:

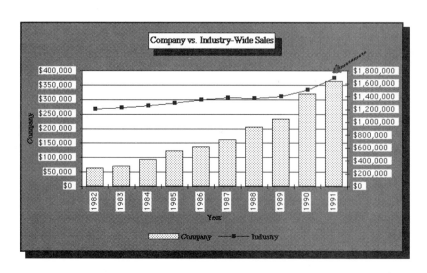

Formatting Text

You can add text anywhere on a chart.

To add unattached text to a chart, just start typing, and your text appears in the formula bar. When you click the enter box or press ENTER, the text appears in the chart. You can move the text anywhere in the chart and format it just as you format any other text.

Add unattached text

You'll add the text "Market share gain" to the chart and use it to label the arrow.

1 Type **Market share gain**

2 Click the enter box or press ENTER.

You still need to move and format the text. Your chart should look like this:

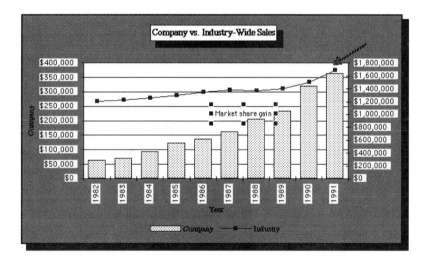

Move the text

Move the text next to the arrow.

▶ Drag the text up and right.

Format the text

Change the color, size, and style of the text with the Format Font command.

1 With the text still selected, choose Format Font.

2 In the Size box, type **9**

3 Under Style, turn on the Italic check box.

4 In the Color list, select blue.

5 Choose the Patterns button.

6 In the Foreground list, select white.

7 Choose OK.

Your finished chart looks like this:

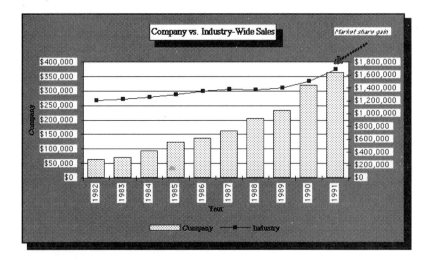

Save and close the documents

Save and close the SALES CHART and SALES HISTORY documents.

1 Choose File Close All.

2 Choose the Yes button to save your changes in each document.

You Try It

In Lesson 13, you created 3-D charts comparing the number of personnel and total of salaries for each department within the three West Coast Sales divisions. In this exercise, you will open and format the Salary chart.

1   Open the UTRYIT14 WORKSPACE.

2   Save the UTRYIT14 CHART as **SALARY CHART**

Choose the Yes button to replace the existing SALARY CHART.

3   Label the category (x) axis **Departments**

4   Label the series (y) axis **Divisions**

5   Label the value (z) axis **Salaries**

6   Add an arrow that points to the Printer R and D column and another that points to the Printer Engineering column.

7   Type the following unattached text:

The Printer division currently markets more products than the other two divisions combined.

8   Move the unattached text to the upper-right corner of the chart. Use the handles to resize the box if necessary.

9   Move both arrows to point to the unattached text.

10   Format the unattached text as blue Helvetica 9-point italic, with a shadow border and white foreground.

11   Select the chart area and format it with a shadow border and light gray foreground.

You can compare the SALARY14 CHART with your results. Save and close the charts when you are finished.

Summary and Preview

In this lesson, you learned to:

Select chart objects with the mouse or keyboard   You selected the chart area, plot area, attached and unattached text, and chart objects such as the legend before moving, sizing, and formatting them.

Change fonts and patterns of chart objects   You used the Format Font and Format Pattern commands, as well as the Font and Pattern buttons, to format chart objects and text. You also double-clicked a chart object to open the Format Patterns dialog box.

Move and size chart objects   You moved chart arrows, unattached text, and the chart legend.

Add an arrow to a chart   You used the Chart Add Arrow command to add an arrow to the chart.

Add unattached text to a chart   You typed text in the formula bar to add unattached text to the chart. You then moved and formatted the text.

Save a chart as a template   You saved chart settings and formatting in a chart template.

In the next lesson, you'll learn how to work with chart data series. You'll add worksheet data to an existing chart. You'll also create an xy chart.

Editing Chart Data Series

You will learn to:

- Select a data series on a chart.
- Edit a data series formula to show different data in a chart.
- Add a data series to a chart or delete it from a chart.
- Create an xy chart.

Estimated lesson time: 45 minutes

In this lesson, you will edit the series formula to change, add, and delete the data in your chart. You will also create an xy chart to show the relationship between two data series.

For more information on editing a series formula, see Chapter 12, "Editing a Chart," in the *Microsoft Excel User's Guide*.

Start the lesson

In this lesson, you will create charts using chart templates and the data in the SALES HISTORY and STOCK worksheets. Open the LESSON15 WORKSPACE and rename the LESSON15A and LESSON15B worksheets.

1 Open the LESSON15 WORKSPACE. The LESSON15B worksheet should be active.

2 Save the worksheet as **STOCK**

3 Switch to the LESSON15A worksheet.

4 Save the worksheet as **SALES HISTORY**

Choose the Yes button to replace the existing SALES HISTORY worksheet.

Using a Chart Template

Create a chart from a template

The legend was removed from the SALES CHART TEMPLATE to create the SALES CHART15 TEMPLATE. Use the SALES CHART15 TEMPLATE to create a chart showing only the company sales from 1982 to 1991.

1 On the SALES HISTORY worksheet, select cells C9:D19.

2 Choose File Open.

3 Select SALES CHART15 TEMPLATE.

4 Choose the Open button.

5 Choose File Save As.

6 In the Save Chart As box, type **SALES CHART**

7 Choose the Save button.

Choose the Yes button to replace the existing SALES CHART.

8 Click the zoom box to expand the chart window.

Your chart should look like this:

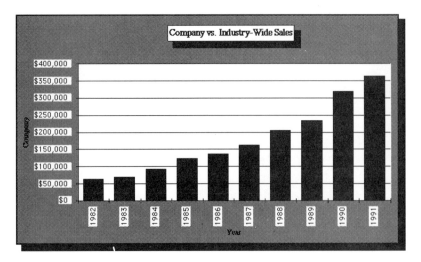

Selecting a Data Series

You can work directly on a chart to change its data.

You can select a data series on a chart by selecting any of its data markers with the mouse or keyboard. When you select a data series, the data series formula is displayed in the formula bar.

Select the company data series

▶ Click one of the columns on the chart.

The series formula appears in the formula bar.

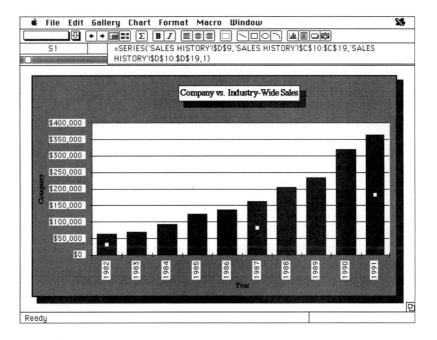

Parts of a series formula   Here's a closer look at the series formula you see in the formula bar.

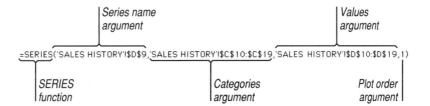

The SERIES function is used to build the series formula. It is used only on charts. The arguments to the SERIES function are external references to the worksheet cells that contain the data. The arguments are:

- **Series name**   This is the Company data series, and cell D9 on the SALES HISTORY worksheet contains the name "Company."

- **Categories**   This argument refers to the cells on the SALES HISTORY worksheet that contain the years 1982 through 1991.

- **Values**   This argument refers to the cells on the SALES HISTORY worksheet that contain the company sales data.

- **Plot order**   This is the order in which the data series is plotted on the chart. Since you have only one data series, the plot order argument is 1.

Adding a Data Series

You add a data series to a chart by selecting cells in the worksheet and pasting them into the chart with Edit Copy and Edit Paste.

Add the industry data series to the chart

Select the cells for the industry data series and paste them into the chart.

1 Switch to the SALES HISTORY worksheet.

2 Select cells E9:E19.

3 Choose Edit Copy.

4 Switch to SALES CHART.

5 Choose Edit Paste.

Your chart should look like this:

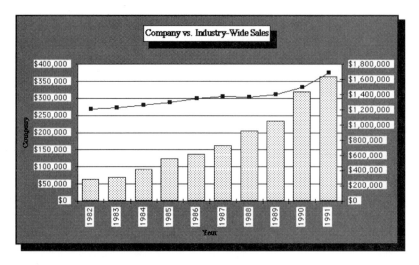

Adding Points to Existing Data Series

You can select a data series in a chart and edit the series formula to change the data included in the chart. You can create or edit a series formula in the formula bar by typing or pointing, just like any other formula. You can also use the Chart Edit Series command to edit the data series in a dialog box.

The Chart Edit Series command You can use the Chart Edit Series command to enter, edit, or delete a data series in a chart. To edit a series, you select the series in the Series box and make the changes in the Name, X, Y, Z, and Plot Order boxes. To delete a data series, select the data series in the chart, choose the Chart Edit Series command, choose the Delete button, and then choose OK.

Add the 1992 data

You'll select the company data series and then edit the category and value arguments to include the cells that contain the year 1992 and company sales for 1992.

1 Select a column on the chart.

2 Choose the Chart Edit Series command.

> ☑ To get Help on the Chart Edit Series command, press COMMAND+ SHIFT+QUESTION MARK while the Chart Edit Series dialog box is displayed.

3 In the Series box, Company should be selected.

4 In the X Labels box, edit the text to SALES HISTORY!$C$10:$C$20.

5 In the Y Values box, edit the text to SALES HISTORY!$D$10:$D$20.

6 Choose the Define button.

7 In the Series box, select Industry.

8 In the Y Values box, edit the text to SALES HISTORY!$E$10:$E$20.

9 Choose OK.

The 1992 figures are added to the chart. Your chart should look like this:

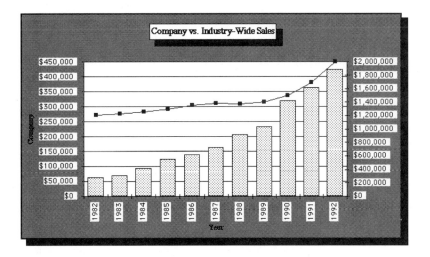

Deleting and Moving a Data Series

You can delete a data series from a chart by using the Delete button in the Chart Edit Series dialog box or by selecting the series formula in the formula bar and choosing Edit Clear or Edit Cut. You can also use Edit Cut and Edit Paste to move a data series to another chart.

Save and close the chart and its supporting worksheet

You have finished the SALES HISTORY worksheet and the SALES CHART. Next, you'll create an xy chart using the STOCK worksheet.

1 Choose File Close to close the chart.

2 Choose the Yes button to save your changes.

3 Choose File Close to close the SALES HISTORY worksheet.

4 Choose the Yes button to save your changes.

Creating an XY (Scatter) Chart

An xy (scatter) chart is different from other charts because it has two sets of values and no categories.

You use an xy chart to plot two sets of numbers to see the relationship between them. One easy way to create an xy chart is to select rows or columns of data only.

Create an xy chart

You will create an xy chart that examines the relationship between the Dow Jones Industrial Averages and the fair market value of West Coast Sales stock.

1 On the STOCK worksheet, choose Formula Goto.

2 Select Dow_vs_WCS.

3 Choose OK.

4 Choose File New.

5 Select Chart.

6 Choose OK.

7 Under First Column Contains, select the Category (X) Axis Labels option.

8 Choose OK.

Your chart should look like this:

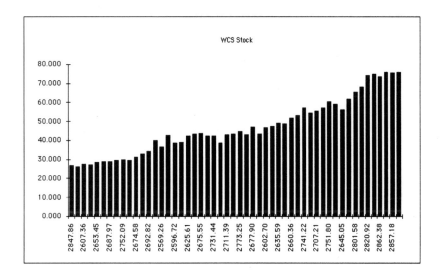

Save the chart

1 Choose <u>F</u>ile Save <u>A</u>s.

2 In the Save Chart As box, type **STOCKXY**

3 Choose the Save button.

Change the chart format

1 Choose <u>G</u>allery XY (<u>S</u>catter).

2 In the XY (Scatter) gallery, select format 3.

3 Choose OK.

Your chart should look like this:

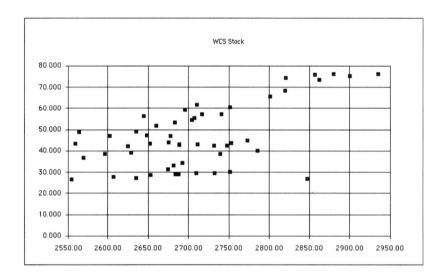

Edit the chart title

When you created the chart, Microsoft Excel used the name of the y-axis
data series as the chart title. You will select and edit the chart title.

1 Select the chart title.

2 In the formula bar, position the insertion point after WCS Stock.

3 Type **vs. Dow Jones Industrial Averages**

4 Click the enter box or press ENTER.

Format the chart title

1 Choose Format Font.

2 In the Font box, select Times.

3 In the Size box, select 12.

4 Under Style, turn on the Bold check box.

5 Choose the Patterns button.

6 Under Border, select the Automatic option.

7 Turn on the Shadow check box.

8 Choose OK.

Attach text to the y axis

1 Choose Chart Attach Text.
2 Under Attach Text To, select the Value (Y) Axis option.
3 Choose OK.
4 In the formula bar, type **WCS Stock Prices**
5 Click the enter box or press ENTER.

Attach text to the x axis

1 Choose Chart Attach Text.
2 Under Attach Text To, select the Category (X) Axis option.
3 Choose OK.
4 In the formula bar, type **Dow Jones Industrial Averages**
5 Click the enter box or press ENTER.

Your finished xy chart looks like this:

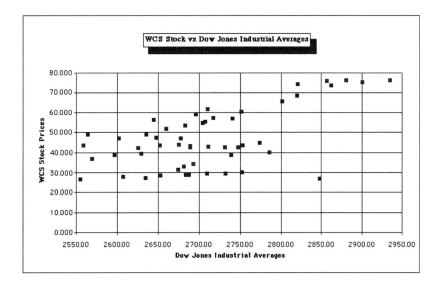

Printing the chart   When you print a chart, the options in the File Page Setup dialog box change. There are no options for printing gridlines and row and column headings, and there's an extra option for setting the size of your printed chart.

Save and close the chart

You will use the STOCK worksheet for the "You Try It" exercise.

1 Choose File Save to save the chart.

2 Choose File Close.

You Try It

In this exercise, you will create a chart using the date on the x axis to compare the performance of the West Coast Sales stock with the Dow Jones Industrial Average. You will use the combination chart template that you created in Lesson 14. You will select all three data series on the STOCK worksheet, open the chart template, edit the data series so that West Coast Sales stock prices are on the left, and then change the title and attached text to reflect the data series you are currently using with the template.

1 In the STOCK worksheet, use the Formula Goto command to select Week_Dow_WCS, the area you will plot in a chart.

2 Open the SALES CHART15 TEMPLATE.

3 Save the chart as **STOCK CHART**

4 Choose Chart Edit Series.

5 Change the plot order of the WCS_Stock series to 1.

6 Change the chart title to **WCS Stock vs. Dow Jones Performance, 7/89-7/90**

7 Change the y-axis label to **WCS Stock Prices**

8 Change the x-axis label to **Week Ending**

9 Change the chart type to combination chart type 3.

10 Use arrows and unattached text to label the WCS Stock and Dow Jones Industrial Average data series.

You can use the Chart Add Legend command to help you identify the data marker that represents the series. Use Chart Delete Legend to delete the legend when you are finished.

Your finished chart should look like this:

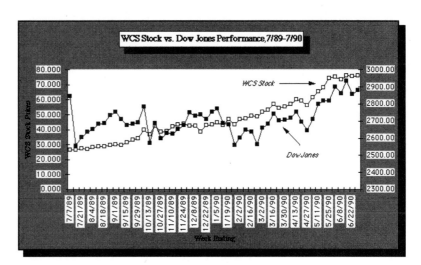

Close the chart and worksheet when you are finished.

Summary and Preview

In this lesson, you learned to:

Select a data series on a chart   You selected a data series by selecting a marker on the chart with either the mouse or keyboard.

Edit a data series formula to show different data in a chart   You used the Chart Edit Series command to change category and value ranges in a series formula.

Add a data series to a chart or delete it from a chart   You used the Edit Copy and Edit Paste commands to add a data series to a chart. You also used the Chart Edit Series command to add a point to an existing data series.

Create an xy chart   You created an xy chart by selecting two columns of data on a worksheet and specifying the first column for the x axis. You then chose the Gallery XY (Scatter) command to change the chart type.

In the next lesson, you'll format a worksheet with an embedded chart and graphics for a presentation.

Using Embedded Charts and Worksheet Graphics

You will learn to:

- Add graphic objects to a worksheet.
- Format graphic objects.
- Add text boxes to a worksheet.
- Create a picture chart.

Estimated lesson time: 45 minutes

In this lesson, you will create a worksheet presentation that combines worksheet data, embedded charts, graphic objects, and text boxes. Combining graphic objects and charts with worksheet data helps you to create a more effective presentation.

For more information on using graphic objects in worksheets, see Chapter 14, "Using Graphics on Microsoft Excel Worksheets," in the *Microsoft Excel User's Guide.*

Start the lesson

You will use the LESSON16 worksheet to create a presentation that depicts the Printer division market share increase since 1982. Open the LESSON16 worksheet and rename it PRESENTATION.

1　Open the LESSON16 worksheet.

2　Save the file as **PRESENTATION**

Wrap the column title text

The Market Share title is wider than the data in the Market Share column. You will adjust the column width and then wrap the Market Share column title text to improve the worksheet's appearance.

1　Select cell E13.

2　Choose Forma<u>t</u> <u>A</u>lignment.

3　Turn on the Wrap Text check box.

4　Choose OK.

Your worksheet should look like this:

	A	B	C	D	E	F	G	H	I
1	West Coast Sales Technologies								
2	Printer Division								
3									
4	*A decade of growth*								
5									
6									
7									
8									
9									
10									
11									
12									
13		Year	Company	Industry	Market Share				
14		1982	$62,947	$1,210,000	4.94%				
15		1983	$69,941	$1,230,000	5.38%				
16		1984	$93,254	$1,260,000	6.89%				
17		1985	$124,339	$1,300,000	8.73%				
18		1986	$138,155	$1,350,000	9.28%				
19		1987	$162,535	$1,380,000	10.54%				
20		1988	$205,740	$1,370,000	13.06%				
21		1989	$233,796	$1,400,000	14.31%				
22		1990	$320,268	$1,500,000	17.59%				
23		1991	$363,941	$1,690,000	17.72%				
24		1992	$423,187	$2,000,000	17.46%				
25									
26									
27									
28									

Laying Out a Worksheet with Charts

You added a chart to a worksheet in Lesson 13. In this lesson, you'll add two pie charts to the worksheet to emphasize the company's increase in market share. To lay out the page properly, you'll use the worksheet gridlines to guide the size and placement of your charts. You'll also use the Gallery Set Preferred command to create a second pie chart that is formatted the same way as the first chart.

Embed a chart in the worksheet

1 Choose Options Display.

Use gridlines as a guide for creating objects.

2 Under Cells, turn on the Gridlines check box.

3 Choose OK.

4 Select cells B14:D14.

5 Click the chart tool in the tool bar.

6 Hold the COMMAND key and drag from cell G14 to cell I24.

Pressing COMMAND while dragging aligns an object with the worksheet grid.

Microsoft Excel creates a column chart. Your worksheet should look like this:

	A	B	C	D	E	F	G	H	I
10									
11									
12									
13		Year	Company	Industry	Market Share			1982	
14		1982	$62,947	$1,210,000	4.94%				
15		1983	$69,941	$1,230,000	5.38%				
16		1984	$93,254	$1,260,000	6.89%		$1,500,000		
17		1985	$124,339	$1,300,000	8.73%		$1,000,000		
18		1986	$138,155	$1,350,000	9.28%				
19		1987	$162,535	$1,380,000	10.54%		$500,000		
20		1988	$205,740	$1,370,000	13.06%		$0		
21		1989	$233,796	$1,400,000	14.31%			1	2
22		1990	$320,268	$1,500,000	17.59%				
23		1991	$363,941	$1,690,000	17.72%				
24		1992	$423,187	$2,000,000	17.46%				
25									

Change the chart type

You selected a single data series for your chart. Change the chart to a 3-D pie chart to compare the company revenues to the industry revenues.

1 Double-click the embedded chart.

Your chart appears in a chart window.

2 Choose Gallery 3-D Pie.

3 In the 3-D Pie gallery, select the third format.

4 Choose OK.

Your chart should look like this:

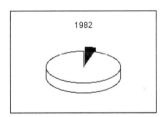

Format the chart title

1 Select the chart title.

2 In the formula bar, type **Fiscal Year 1982**

3 Click the enter box or press ENTER.

4 With the title still selected, choose Format Font.

5 In the Size box, select 12.

6 Under Style, turn on the Bold and Italic check boxes.

7 Choose the Patterns button.

8 Under Border, turn on the Shadow check box.

9 Under Area, select the third pattern from the Pattern list.

10 Choose OK.

Format the Industry data point

You will change the pattern of the pie section that represents the industry.

1 Select the large pie section, the data point representing the industry.

2 Choose Format Patterns.

3 Under Area, select cyan from the Foreground list. Cyan is the eighth option in the list.

4 In the Pattern list, select the fourth pattern option.

5 Choose OK.

Format the company data point

Now you will change the pattern of the pie section that represents the company.

1 Select the small slice of the pie, the data point representing the company.

2 Choose Format Patterns.

3 Under Area, select the third pattern from the Pattern list.

4 Choose OK.

Your chart should look like this:

The preferred chart type   The preferred chart type is the chart type that appears when you create a new chart with the File New command. The Microsoft Excel preferred chart type is a column chart. If you create another type of chart you want to use again in the same session, save time by creating and saving your own preferred chart type.

You can save all of your chart formatting, including titles, with your preferred chart and quickly produce several charts formatted alike.

The Gallery Set Preferred command   With Gallery Set Preferred, you can change the default format that Microsoft Excel uses when you create a new chart. To change the preferred chart format, format the active chart the way you want it and then choose Gallery Set Preferred.

The Gallery Preferred command   With Gallery Preferred, you can change the active chart to the preferred chart format. If you change the active chart and then decide you want to return to the original chart format, choose Gallery Preferred.

Set the preferred chart type

You created a 3-D pie chart that represents the company's market share for 1982. Rather than repeating all the formatting procedures, set the active chart as the preferred chart type. When you create your next chart, the chart type and formatting will already be set.

▶ Choose Gallery Set Preferred.

Close the chart window

You've finished creating the first chart. Now you will add another pie chart to the worksheet.

▶ Close the chart window.

Embed a second pie chart in the worksheet

You will create a pie chart representing the 1992 data series. It will use the same chart type and formatting as the Fiscal Year 1982 chart. Create the new chart and edit the chart title.

1 Select cells B24:D24.

2 Click the chart tool in the tool bar.

3 Hold the COMMAND key and drag from cell G26 to cell I36.

4 Double-click the embedded chart to open a chart window.

5 Select the chart title.

6 In the formula bar, change the title to **Fiscal Year 1992**

7 Click the enter box or press ENTER.

8 Close the chart window.

Your worksheet should look like this:

	A	B	C	D	E	F	G	H	I
13		Year	Company	Industry	Market Share				
14		1982	$62,947	$1,210,000	4.94%				
15		1983	$69,941	$1,230,000	5.38%			Fiscal Year 1982	
16		1984	$93,254	$1,260,000	6.89%				
17		1985	$124,339	$1,300,000	8.73%				
18		1986	$138,155	$1,350,000	9.28%				
19		1987	$162,535	$1,380,000	10.54%				
20		1988	$205,740	$1,370,000	13.06%				
21		1989	$233,796	$1,400,000	14.31%				
22		1990	$320,268	$1,500,000	17.59%				
23		1991	$363,941	$1,690,000	17.72%				
24		1992	$423,187	$2,000,000	17.46%				
25									
26									
27								Fiscal Year 1992	
28									
29									
30									
31									
32									
33									
34									
35									
36									
37									

Move the charts on the worksheet

You will rearrange the charts on the worksheet to make room for text boxes and arrows. Select the charts and drag them where you want them. Use the worksheet gridlines as guides for placement of the charts.

1 Select the Fiscal Year 1982 chart.

2 Hold the COMMAND key and drag the chart to cell G6.

The chart should be in the cell range G6:I15.

3 Select the Fiscal Year 1992 chart.

4 Hold the COMMAND key and drag the chart to cell G23.

The chart should be within the cell range G23:I33.

The selection tool You can use the selection tool to select multiple worksheet objects at once. Click the selection tool, point to the first object you want to select, and then drag the pointer over the remaining objects you want in the selection. Each selected object is marked by selection squares.

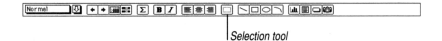

Selection tool

Remove the chart borders

You want the 3-D pie charts to appear on the worksheet without borders.

1 Click the selection tool in the tool bar.

2 Point above and to the left of the Fiscal Year 1982 chart and drag down below the Fiscal Year 1992 chart, so that both charts are enclosed by the selection marquee.

Both charts are surrounded by selection handles.

3 Choose Format Patterns.

4 Under Border, select the None option.

5 Choose OK.

Turn off the gridlines

Use the Options Display command to turn off the gridlines again.

1 Choose Options Display.

2 Under Cells, turn off the Gridlines check box.

3 Choose OK.

Your worksheet should look like this:

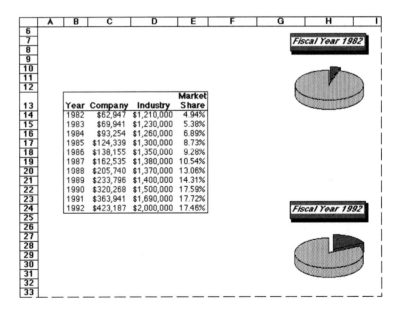

Drawing Lines and Shapes on the Worksheet

Drawing graphic objects You can add emphasis to your worksheet or macro sheet with graphic objects such as straight lines, ovals, rectangles, and arcs. By adding arrowheads to straight lines, you can use them to point to cells, charts, other graphic objects, or copied pictures. You can also fill ovals, rectangles, and arcs with a color and pattern to highlight certain areas of the document. As you learned in the previous procedure, you can align graphic objects with the worksheet grid. You can also restrict the graphic object to certain shapes by pressing the SHIFT key while drawing the object.

To draw a	Press the SHIFT key while drawing a
Square	Rectangle
Circle	Oval
Horizontal, vertical, or 45-degree angle line	Line

Formatting object placement You can use the Format Object Placement command to align the object on the worksheet. You can use this command to maintain an object's position relative to the cells at the upper-left and lower-right corners; to move the object with the cell under its upper-left corner without changing size; or to fix the object's position so it doesn't move with the cells at all.

Add arrows to the worksheet

Add lines to the worksheet and format them as arrows. The arrows will point from the 1982 and 1992 worksheet data to the pie charts representing that data.

1 Click the line tool in the tool bar.

2 Drag from the right border of cell E14, the 1982 data, to the left of the pie slice on the Fiscal Year 1982 pie chart.

3 Choose Format Patterns.

4 Under Line, select the third line weight from the Weight list.

5 Under Arrow Head, select the last style from the Style list.

6 In the Width list, select the first width.

7 Choose OK.

Your worksheet should look like this:

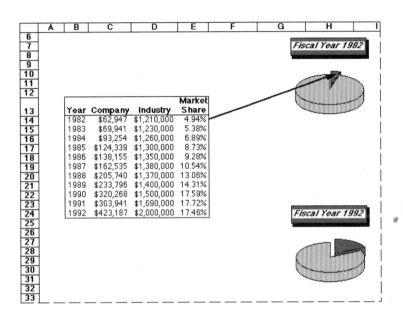

	Year	Company	Industry	Market Share
13				
14	1982	$62,947	$1,210,000	4.94%
15	1983	$69,941	$1,230,000	5.38%
16	1984	$93,254	$1,260,000	6.89%
17	1985	$124,339	$1,300,000	8.73%
18	1986	$138,155	$1,350,000	9.28%
19	1987	$162,535	$1,380,000	10.54%
20	1988	$205,740	$1,370,000	13.06%
21	1989	$233,796	$1,400,000	14.31%
22	1990	$320,268	$1,500,000	17.59%
23	1991	$303,941	$1,690,000	17.72%
24	1992	$423,187	$2,000,000	17.46%

Copy the arrow

You will copy and paste a second arrow in the worksheet. To do this, select
the arrow, choose Edit Copy, and choose Edit Paste. Drag either end of the
arrow where you want it to point. In this procedure you will copy, paste, and
move the arrow between the 1992 data series and the Fiscal Year 1992 chart.

1 If the arrow is not still selected, click it.

2 Choose Edit Copy.

3 Choose Edit Paste.

   The pasted arrow is located on top of the original arrow.

4 Drag the arrow by the shaft to the right border of cell E24.

5 Drag the arrowhead to the left of the pie slice on the Fiscal Year 1992 pie
   chart.

Your worksheet should look like this:

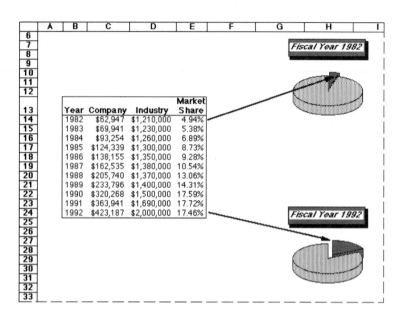

Adding Text Boxes to the Worksheet

You can use text boxes to add titles, footnotes, and comments about cell data.

Adding text boxes You use the text box tool in the tool bar to draw text boxes on your worksheet. Draw a text box just as you draw any other graphic object, by clicking the tool and dragging across the worksheet. To add text to the text box, click inside the text box and type the text. You can change the fonts, style, size, and color of the text with the Format Font command. One text box can contain multiple fonts, styles, and colors. You can also use the Format Patterns command to change the fill pattern or borders of a text box.

Text box tool

Add a text box to the worksheet

Use a text box to add a title to the worksheet data.

1   Click the text box tool in the tool bar.

2   Hold COMMAND and drag from the upper-left corner of cell B9 to the lower-right corner of cell F11.

3   If the insertion point is not in the text box, click inside the text box.

4   Type **Printer Division Revenues**

Format the title

Change the font and alignment of the title.

1   Select the text you just entered.

2   Choose Format Font.

3   In the Size box, select 18.

4   Under Style, turn on the Bold and Italic check boxes.

5   In the Color list, select dark blue.

6   Choose OK.

Your worksheet should look like this:

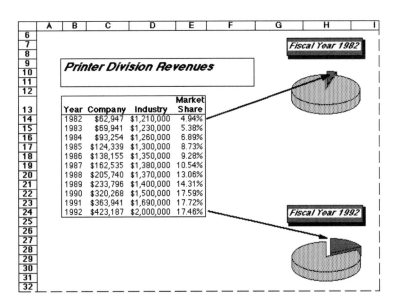

Add footnotes to the revenue table

You will use a text box to add footnotes to the revenue table.

1 Click the text box tool in the tool bar.

2 Hold COMMAND and drag from cell B26 to cell F28.

3 In the text box, type the following text:

   * Revenue in thousands of dollars

   * Industry figures exclusive of WCS revenues

Format the footnotes

1 Select the text you just entered.

2 Choose Format Font.

3 Under Style, turn on the Italic check box.

4 In the Color list, select dark blue.

5 Choose the Patterns button.

6 Under Border, select the None option.

7 Choose OK.

Format the title

You want the title for the revenue data to stand out. You will format the border and the fill pattern.

1 Click the border of the "Printer Division Revenues" text box to select it.

   ❓ For information on formatting text box borders, see online Help. Choose Window Help, select the Worksheet Procedures topic, and scroll to the Formatting Text Box Borders and Fill Patterns topic.

2 Choose Format Patterns.

3 Under Border, select the second option from the Weight list.

4 Turn on the Round Corners check box.

5 Under Fill, select the third pattern from the Pattern list.

6 Choose OK.

7 With the text box still selected, drag the handle on the right side of the box to the left so that the box is just wide enough to contain the text.

Your worksheet should look like this:

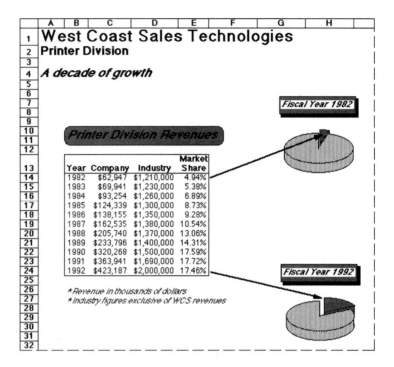

Save the worksheet

▶ Choose File Save.

Set up the page to print the worksheet

You will use the File Page Setup command to set up the page for printing.

1 Choose File Page Setup.

2 Change the header, footer, margins, gridlines, and orientation settings to those shown in the following illustration.

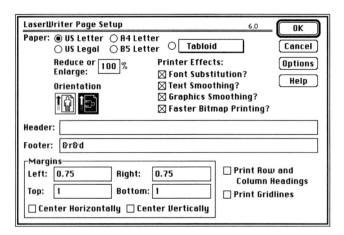

3 Choose OK.

Preview the worksheet before printing

You will use the File Print Preview command to see how the document will look when printed. You can also print the worksheet now.

1 Choose File Print Preview.

The Print Preview window should look like the following illustration. Yours may look different, depending on the printer driver you have installed.

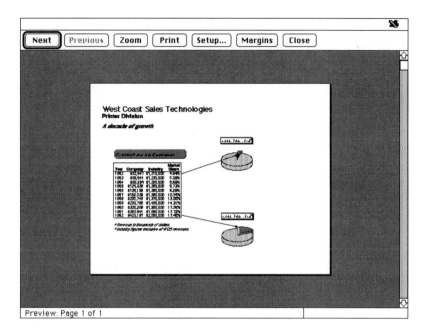

2   If you want to print the worksheet now, choose the Print button.

Otherwise, choose the Close button to close the preview window.

Creating Picture Charts

You can use pictures that were created in other applications as data markers in Microsoft Excel charts.

Using pictures as data markers   You can create unique charts by using pictures as data markers. Select a picture in another application and choose the Edit Copy command. Open your chart, select a data marker, and then choose the Edit Paste command. The data series marker is replaced by the picture.

Formatting a data marker picture   You can format the picture data markers as stacked or stretched. Select the picture data marker, choose the Format Patterns command, and select the Stretch, Stack, or Stack And Scale To option. Use the Stretch option to stretch or shrink the picture to show different values; the Stack option to stack copies of the picture to represent different values; or the Stack And Scale To option to stack copies of the picture and scale each picture to a value you specify.

Create a new chart

You will create a picture chart to use with the worksheet that you just formatted. You will use the data in the PRESENTATION worksheet to create a combination chart with the SALES CHART16 TEMPLATE.

1 On the PRESENTATION worksheet, select cells B13:D24.

2 Choose File Open.

3 Select SALES CHART16 TEMPLATE.

4 Choose the Open button.

5 Choose File Save As.

6 In the Save Chart As box, type **PRINTER CHART**

7 Choose the Save button.

Copy a picture to the company data marker

You will replace the company data marker with a picture. To do this you will copy a picture from another worksheet, PRINTER ART16, and paste it into PRINTER CHART.

1 Choose File Open.

2 Select PRINTER ART16.

3 Choose the Open button.

4 On the PRINTER ART16 worksheet, select the picture labeled Graphic.

5 Choose Edit Copy.

6 Switch to PRINTER CHART.

7 Select the Company data markers (the column markers).

8 Choose Edit Paste.

The printer graphic replaces the company data markers. Your chart should look like this:

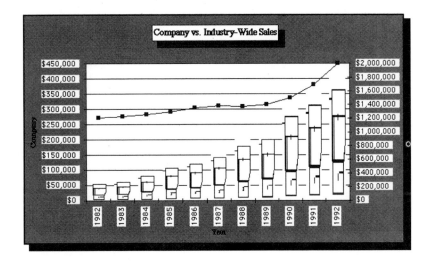

Format the data marker pictures

Use the Format Patterns command to stack and scale the data marker pictures.

1 On the chart, select a Company data marker.

2 Choose Format Patterns.

3 Under Picture Format, select the Stack And Scale To option.

4 In the Units/Picture box, type 50,000.

5 Choose OK.

Your chart should look like this:

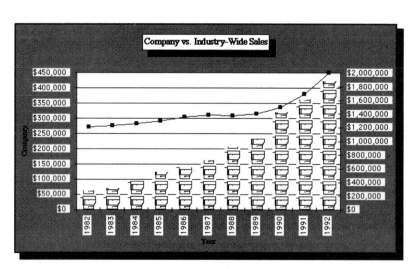

Save and close the chart window

Save and close PRINTER CHART and close the PRINTER ART16 worksheet. You will use the PRESENTATION worksheet in the "You Try It" exercise.

1 Choose File Save.

2 Choose File Close.

3 Switch to the PRINTER ART16 worksheet.

4 Choose File Close.

Using Microsoft Excel Graphics with Other Applications

You can export worksheet data or objects into another application. You can copy these items or pictures of these items into a graphical word processing or presentation application, such as Microsoft® Word or Microsoft® PowerPoint®. To import data into Microsoft Word and link it to Microsoft Excel, select the chart, graphic, or worksheet cells you want to copy, choose Edit Copy, switch to Microsoft Word, and choose Edit Paste Link. If you make changes to the original Microsoft Excel data, you can update the pasted data in Microsoft Word with the Edit Update Link command.

To import a picture into Microsoft PowerPoint, select the chart, graphic, or worksheet cells you want to copy, hold down SHIFT, and choose Edit Copy Picture. If you are copying a chart, you will be asked whether you want to copy the chart as it appears on the screen or as printed. If your computer is set up with a color printer, select the As Shown When Printed option. Otherwise, select the As Shown On Screen option. Switch to Microsoft PowerPoint and choose Edit Paste.

You Try It

In this lesson, you created a worksheet with embedded charts, arrows, and text boxes. In this exercise, you will use the rectangle tool to add bars at the top and bottom of the worksheet. To do this you will change row heights at the top and bottom of the worksheet, click the rectangle tool, and draw rectangles at the top and bottom of the document. You will then format the rectangles as bars.

1   On the PRESENTATION worksheet, change the row height of row 3 to 20 points.

2   Change the row height of row 34 to 6 points.

3   Hold the COMMAND key and click the rectangle tool in the tool bar.

Pressing the COMMAND key while clicking the tool enables you to draw multiple objects.

4   Hold the COMMAND key and drag from cell A3 to cell F3.

5   Hold the COMMAND key and drag from cell A34 to cell F34.

6   Select both rectangles. Select the first rectangle and then press SHIFT while you select the second one.

7   Choose Format Patterns.

8   Under Borders, select the None option.

9   Under Fill, select dark cyan in the Foreground list (the third from last color).

10   Choose OK.

Your worksheet should look like this:

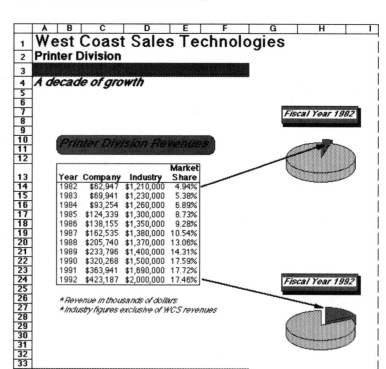

Your worksheet is complete. Save and close the worksheet.

Summary and Preview

In this lesson, you learned to:

Add graphic objects to a worksheet   You used the line and rectangle tools in the tool bar to add graphics to your report.

Format graphic objects   You formatted graphic objects with the Format Patterns command.

Add text boxes to a worksheet   You added text boxes to the report, and then typed and formatted text in these boxes.

Create a picture chart   You copied a picture from another document and used it to replace a data marker. You then formatted the picture data marker as stacked.

In the next lesson, you will record macros with the macro recorder. You'll edit these macros and assign them to buttons on the worksheet so that you can click the buttons to run the macros.

6 Working with Macros

Recording Macros

You will learn to:

- Record a macro.
- Understand a macro sheet.
- Edit and document a macro.
- Run a macro.
- Interrupt a macro.
- Step through a macro.
- Assign macros to worksheet buttons.

Estimated lesson time: 45 minutes

Microsoft Excel has a macro recorder to help you create macros.

In this lesson, you will use the Microsoft Excel macro recorder to automate work you do regularly. You'll find out how macro sheets differ from worksheets. You'll learn techniques for documenting macros, so that they're easier to read and understand. You'll run a macro, and learn how to test it by running it one step at a time. You'll also create worksheet buttons, assign macros to the buttons, and run the macros by clicking the buttons.

In this lesson, you'll create a small application in Microsoft Excel. The application will make it easy for you to update a worksheet, print the worksheet data, and plot the data in a chart by clicking a worksheet button.

Start the lesson

Open the LESSON17 worksheet, rename it WCS SALES, and arrange the worksheet to fill the screen.

1 Open LESSON17.

2 Save the worksheet as **WCS SALES**

3 Close any other open windows, and choose Window Arrange All.

Define the area as a database

By taking advantage of Microsoft Excel database features, you can write shorter macros to update and print the data and plot it in a chart. Use the Data Set Database command to define the range where you'll enter data as a database. Microsoft Excel names the selected cells "Database."

1 Select cells C9:F20.

2 Choose Data Set Database.

Now your worksheet is set up for your application, and you're ready to start creating a macro.

Recording a Macro as You Work

With the Microsoft Excel macro recorder, you can easily create a macro that automates your tasks. Just start the macro recorder, go through your tasks, and then stop the macro recorder. Microsoft Excel records your actions as a macro on a macro sheet. You can run the macro whenever you want to repeat the tasks.

Macro Record automatically records your actions on the macro sheet.

The Macro Record command   With Macro Record, you can start recording a macro without any preparation at all. Macro Record opens a new macro sheet and then prompts you to enter a macro name and optional shortcut key. You don't need to look at the macro sheet until you finish recording your tasks.

Start recording a macro

Use the Macro Record command to start recording a macro that updates the WCS SALES worksheet data. You'll name the macro "Update" and give it the keyboard shortcut COMMAND+OPTION+U.

If you make a mistake while recording a macro, keep going. You can edit the macro later to remove unnecessary steps.

1 Choose Macro Record.

2 In the Name box, type **Update**

3 In the Option+⌘ Key box, type **u**

4 Choose OK.

Display the data form

You won't change any data right now. Just choose the Data Form command so that the data form is displayed when you run the Update macro. Then close the data form without making any changes.

1 Choose Data Form.

2 Choose the Close button.

The Macro Stop Recorder command   Macro Stop Recorder turns off the macro recorder.

Stop the macro recorder

You have finished recording the Update macro. Stop recording your actions by choosing the Macro Stop Recorder command.

▶ Choose Macro Stop Recorder.

Understanding Macro Sheets

Microsoft Excel macros are stored on a macro sheet.

Now you'll see how macro sheets differ from worksheets.

Save the new macro sheet

1 Switch to Macro1.

2 Choose File Save As.

3 In the Save Macro As box, type **SALES MACRO**

4 Choose the Save button.

Your macro sheet should look like this:

	A	B
1	Update (u)	
2	=DATA.FORM()	
3	=RETURN()	
4		

If you didn't follow the steps exactly, your macro sheet may look slightly different from the illustration. You can edit the macro sheet to make it match the illustration.

Microsoft Excel macros record formulas for the steps you followed.

Macros display formulas instead of values   Macro sheets usually display formulas, while worksheets usually display values. Macros are made up of formulas you write and Microsoft Excel functions, so it's more important to see formulas in a macro sheet.

Macro functions and worksheet functions   Microsoft Excel has two types of functions, worksheet functions and macro functions. You can use worksheet functions on a worksheet or a macro sheet, but you can use macro functions only on a macro sheet. DATA.FORM and RETURN are examples of macro functions.

The Options Display command   With Options Display, you can control whether a worksheet or macro sheet displays values or formulas.

Change the display from formulas to values

Displaying values returned by your macro functions is useful when you're testing a macro. You can also use a keyboard shortcut to alternate between displaying formulas and displaying values.

1 Choose Options Display.

2 Under Cells, turn off the Formulas check box.

3 Choose OK.

    ◈   You can also press COMMAND+` (left single quotation mark) to switch between display of formulas and values.

Your macro sheet should look like this. Each macro function returns the value FALSE, because the functions haven't been calculated yet.

	A	B	C
1	Update (u)		
2	FALSE		
3	FALSE		
4			

Calculation when you run the macro vs. automatic calculation   Another difference between macro sheets and worksheets is that the formulas and functions in a macro sheet are calculated only when you run the macro. The macro is calculated one cell at a time, starting at the top of the macro, following the flow of logic, and ending at the RETURN function.

Change the display from values to formulas

Change the display back to formulas so you can see the macro functions again.

1   Choose Options Display.

2   Under Cells, turn on the Formulas check box.

3   Choose OK.

> ✐   You can also press COMMAND+` instead of doing steps 1 through 3.

Defining a macro name   When you choose Formula Define Name on a macro sheet, the Formula Define Name dialog box contains an extra box for defining macro names. When you write a macro on the macro sheet instead of using the recorder, you choose Formula Define Name to name the macro, specify whether it is a command macro or a custom function, and assign a shortcut key if it is a command macro. You used a custom function to convert Fahrenheit to Celsius in Lesson 8, "Advanced Worksheet Features."

Display the names in the macro sheet

Choose the Formula Define Name command to see the names that the macro recorder defined in your macro sheet.

1   Choose Formula Define Name.

The Formula Define Name dialog box looks like this:

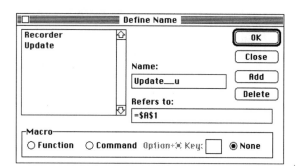

2   Choose the Close button.

Recording a Macro on an Open Macro Sheet

When you choose the Macro Record command without a macro sheet open, Microsoft Excel opens a new macro sheet and records your macro in column A. If you choose Macro Record a second time, the second macro is recorded in column B, and so on.

Once you have an open macro sheet, you may prefer to record a macro in specific cells.

The Macro Set Recorder and Macro Start Recorder commands   With Macro Set Recorder, you can specify where you want the macro recorded in your macro sheet. If you select a single cell, all the cells below that cell in the same column become the recorder range. Once you've specified where you want to record the macro, you can choose Macro Start Recorder to start recording your macro.

Action-equivalent functions   Whenever you use the macro recorder, you create a macro made up of action-equivalent functions. All the functions in the recorded macro represent actions that you can also perform manually in Microsoft Excel.

Record a short macro to activate the worksheet

You want the WCS SALES worksheet to be active whenever you run the Update macro. You can use the macro recorder to record the action-equivalent function to activate the WCS SALES worksheet. Set the macro recorder to start recording in cell A5.

1 Select cell A5.

2 Choose Macro Set Recorder.

3 Choose Macro Start Recorder.

4 Choose Window WCS SALES.

5 Choose Macro Stop Recorder.

6 Switch back to the SALES MACRO macro sheet.

Your macro sheet should look like this:

	A	B	C
1	Update (u)		
2	=DATA.FORM()		
3	=RETURN()		
4			
5	=ACTIVATE("WCS SALES")		
6	=RETURN()		
7			

Editing and Documenting Macros

You edit a macro sheet the same way you edit a worksheet. You can edit cell contents in the formula bar, clear cells, move cells, and insert and delete cells. However, if you have macros in many different areas of a macro sheet, you may often need to insert or delete ranges of cells, not entire rows and columns, as you frequently do in worksheets.

Documenting a macro sheet is just as important as documenting a worksheet. Your macro sheet should be presented in an organized way, so that it's easy to understand.

Insert the ACTIVATE function in the Update macro

Move your recorded ACTIVATE function to the beginning of the Update macro, so the Update macro will always start by activating the WCS SALES worksheet.

1 Select cell A5.

2 Choose Edit Cut.

3 Select cell A2.

4 Choose Edit Insert Paste.

Clear the extra RETURN function

The RETURN function ends a macro.

1 Select cell A6.

2 Choose Edit Clear.

3 Choose OK.

Your macro sheet looks like this:

	A	B	C
1	Update (u)		
2	=ACTIVATE("WCS SALES")		
3	=DATA.FORM()		
4	=RETURN()		
5			

Add comments to the macro functions

Now add comments to each of the macro functions so you can remember what the Update macro does.

▶ In column B, type the comments shown in the following illustration:

	A	B	C
1	Update (u)		
2	=ACTIVATE("WCS SALES")	Make sure the worksheet is active	
3	=DATA.FORM()	Display data form	
4	=RETURN()	End macro	
5			

Format and document the macro sheet

It's okay to have blank cells in Microsoft Excel macros.

You'll eventually have other macros on this macro sheet. You'll use column A for cell names, column B for macro statements, and column C for comments. You can widen columns B and C to see more of the cell contents. Remember, to insert three rows, select the three rows you want to move down, and then choose Edit Insert.

▶ Format your macro sheet to look like this:

	A	B	C
1		COMMAND MACROS	
2			
3	Cell Names	Macro name or statement	Shortcut key/Comments
4		Update	(u)
5		=ACTIVATE("WCS SALES")	Make sure the worksheet is active
6		=DATA.FORM()	Display data form
7		=RETURN()	End macro
8			

Running a Macro

When you run a macro, Microsoft Excel calculates the formulas in the macro sheet one cell at a time.

Running a macro with the Macro Run command or the shortcut key   With Macro Run, you can run any command macro that is on an open macro sheet. You can select the name of the macro to run or you can specify the cell in the macro sheet at which to start calculating. You can also run a command macro by pressing the shortcut key you assigned to the macro.

Run the Update macro

Run the Update macro to see how it activates the WCS SALES worksheet and displays the data form. You can use the Macro Run command or press the shortcut keys you assigned to the Update macro, COMMAND+OPTION+U.

1   Choose Macro Run.

2   Select SALES MACRO!Update.

3   Choose OK.

   🖘   You can also press COMMAND+OPTION+U instead of doing steps 1 through 3.

4   Choose the Close button to close the data form.

5   Switch back to the SALES MACRO macro sheet.

Interrupting a Running Macro

Microsoft Excel presents options when you interrupt a macro.

Interrupting a macro   You can interrupt a running macro by pressing COMMAND+PERIOD or ESC. When you interrupt a macro, a dialog box appears. You can choose the Halt button to stop the macro, the Continue button to resume running the macro, or the Step button to run the macro a single statement at a time.

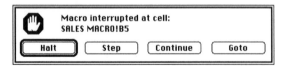

Stepping Through a Macro

The STEP function   Calculating a macro one formula at a time can be useful when you're testing the macro. If you begin your macro with a STEP function, you can run the macro with the Single Step dialog box on the screen.

Add a STEP function to the Update macro

Insert cells at the start of your Update macro and add the STEP function, so you can run the macro by calculating one formula at a time. Instead of typing the STEP function, try pasting it into the macro with the Formula Paste Function command. You can always use Formula Paste Function if you forget the exact name or syntax of a function.

1   Select cells A5:C5.

2   Choose Edit Insert.

3   Choose OK.

4   Select cell B5.

You can select the macro function you want from a list.

5   Choose Formula Paste Function.

6   In the Paste Function box, select STEP( ).

7   Choose OK.

8   Click the enter box or press ENTER.

9   Select cells B5 and C5 and click the bold button in the tool bar to turn off the bold formatting.

10   Type a comment for your STEP function, as shown in the following illustration.

	A	B	C
1		COMMAND MACROS	
2			
3	Cell Names	Macro name or statement	Shortcut key/Comments
4		Update	(u)
5		=STEP()	Calculate one function at a time
6		=ACTIVATE("WCS SALES")	Make sure the worksheet is active
7		=DATA.FORM()	Display data form
8		=RETURN()	End macro
9			

Step through the Update macro

Now when you run your Update macro, it will start by displaying the Single Step dialog box.

1 Choose Macro Run.

2 Select SALES MACRO!Update.

3 Choose OK.

   ✎ You can also press COMMAND+OPTION+U instead of doing steps 1 through 3.

   The Single Step dialog box appears, showing the next formula that will be calculated in your macro.

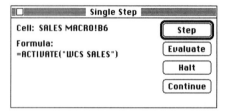

4 Choose the Step button to calculate the next formula.

5 Choose the Halt button to stop running the Update macro.

6 Switch back to SALES MACRO.

Watching Microsoft Excel evaluate a single macro formula   When you're using the Single Step dialog box, you can choose the Evaluate button repeatedly to see how Microsoft Excel evaluates a single macro formula. This is useful for testing long macro statements with many nested functions.

Disable the STEP function in the Update macro

If you delete the equal sign from STEP, Microsoft Excel can't calculate it as a function. Later, if you want to use the STEP function again, you can retype the equal sign.

1 Select cell B5.

2 In the formula bar, change =STEP( ) to STEP( )

3 Click the enter box or press ENTER.

Recording and Naming Another Macro

Now you're ready to create your second macro. The Print macro will display the WCS SALES worksheet in print preview.

Start recording your Print macro

You'll use the Macro Set Recorder and Macro Start Recorder commands to record the macro starting in cell B11.

1   Select cell B11.

2   Choose Macro Set Recorder.

3   Choose Macro Start Recorder.

Record a macro to preview the worksheet data

You'll use Microsoft Excel's database features to set the Database range on the WCS SALES worksheet as the print area. That way, no matter how many rows of data you enter, the macro will preview all of your data.

1   Switch to WCS SALES.

2   Choose Formula Goto.

3   In the Goto box, select Database.

4   Choose OK.

5   Choose Options Set Print Area.

6   Choose File Print Preview.

7   Choose the Close button.

Stop the macro recorder and activate the macro sheet

1   Choose Macro Stop Recorder.

2   Switch to the SALES MACRO macro sheet.

Name the macro "Print"

Use the Formula Define Name command to name your macro "Print," define
it as a command macro, and assign the shortcut key COMMAND+OPTION+P.
You'll also type the macro name in the macro sheet, so it's easy to remember
the name.

1 Select cell B10.

2 Type **Print**

3 Click the enter box or press ENTER.

4 Choose Formula Define Name.

5 Under Macro, select the Command option.

6 In the Option+⌘ Key box, type **p**

7 Choose OK.

Document the Print macro

▶ Format and add comments to your Print macro so it looks like the
following illustration:

	A	B	C
1		COMMAND MACROS	
2			
3	Cell Names	Macro name or statement	Shortcut key/Comments
4		Update	(u)
5		STEP()	Calculate one function at a time
6		=ACTIVATE("WCS SALES")	Make sure the worksheet is active
7		=DATA.FORM()	Display data form
8		=RETURN()	End macro
9			
10		Print	(p)
11		=ACTIVATE("WCS SALES")	Make sure worksheet is active
12		=FORMULA.GOTO("Database")	Select area named "Database"
13		=SET.PRINT.AREA()	Set selection as print area
14		=PRINT.PREVIEW()	Print preview
15		=RETURN()	End macro
16			

Running Macros with Buttons

You can make your macros easier to use by assigning them to buttons or other worksheet objects.

Worksheet buttons   You create a button the same way you create text boxes and other graphic objects. Use the button tool on the tool bar to create a button on the worksheet. When you release the mouse button, the button appears with the text "Button" and Microsoft Excel displays the Assign To Object dialog box. Select the macro you want to assign to the button and choose OK. You can format the text in the button by choosing the Format Font command. If you want to change the font on a button, press the COMMAND key while clicking the button and choose the Format Font command.

Button tool

Splitting the worksheet window and freezing the panes   You can use the Options Freeze Panes command to create an area for buttons that will not scroll up or down with the worksheet.

Create an area for buttons

You will create an area for buttons at the top of the WCS SALES worksheet.

1 Switch to the WCS SALES worksheet.

2 Select rows 1 through 3.

3 Choose Edit Insert.

4 Point to the split box on the scroll bar and drag the horizontal split bar to row 3.

Split box

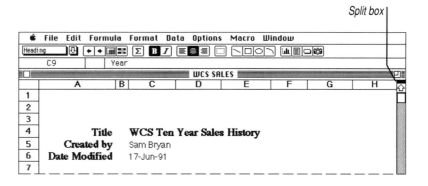

5 Choose Options Freeze Panes.

6 Select row 2.

7 Choose Format Row Height.

8 In the Row Height box, type **18**

9 Choose OK.

Your worksheet should look like this:

	A	B	C	D	E	F	G
1							
2							
3							
4	Title		WCS Ten Year Sales History				
5	Created by		Sam Bryan				
6	Date Modified		17-Jun-91				
7							
8	Purpose		This worksheet summarizes West Coast Sales' gross revenue				
9			for the previous ten years.				
10							
11	Sales History						
12			Year	Company	Industry	% Share	
13			1982	$62,947	$1,210,000	4.94%	
14			1983	$69,941	$1,230,000	5.38%	
15			1984	$93,254	$1,260,000	6.89%	
16			1985	$124,339	$1,300,000	8.73%	
17			1986	$138,155	$1,350,000	9.28%	
18			1987	$162,535	$1,380,000	10.54%	
19			1988	$205,740	$1,370,000	13.06%	
20			1989	$233,796	$1,400,000	14.31%	
21			1990	$320,268	$1,500,000	17.59%	

Create an Update button

Add a button at the top of the worksheet to run the Update macro.

1 Click the button tool in the tool bar.

2 Press the COMMAND key while dragging the pointer across cell C2.

   The button is aligned with cell C2.

3 In the Assign Macro box, select SALES MACRO!Update.

4 Choose OK.

Format the button text

1 With the button still selected, type **Update**

2 Select the button by clicking the border or by pressing COMMAND while clicking the button.

3 Choose Format Font.

4 In the Font box, select Helvetica.

5 Under Style, turn on the Bold and Italic check boxes.

6 Choose OK.

Create a Print button

Add a button at the top of the worksheet to run the Print macro.

1   Click the button tool on the tool bar.

2   Press the COMMAND key while dragging the pointer across cell E2.

The button is aligned with cell E2.

3   In the Assign Macro box, select SALES MACRO!Print.

4   Choose OK.

Format the Print button

1   With the button still selected, type **Print**

2   Select the button by clicking the border or by pressing COMMAND while clicking the button.

3   Choose Format Font.

4   In the Font box, select Helvetica.

5   Under Style, turn on the Bold and Italic check boxes.

6   Choose OK.

Your worksheet should look like this:

	A	B	C	D	E	F	G
1							
2			*Update*		*Print*		
3							
4	**Title**		**WCS Ten Year Sales History**				
5	**Created by**		Sam Bryan				
6	**Date Modified**		17-Jun-91				
7							
8	**Purpose**		This worksheet summarizes West Coast Sales' gross revenue				
9			for the previous ten years.				
10							
11	**Sales History**						
12			Year	Company	Industry	% Share	
13			1982	$62,947	$1,210,000	4.94%	
14			1983	$69,941	$1,230,000	5.38%	
15			1984	$93,254	$1,260,000	6.89%	
16			1985	$124,339	$1,300,000	8.73%	
17			1986	$138,155	$1,350,000	9.28%	
18			1987	$162,535	$1,380,000	10.54%	
19			1988	$205,740	$1,370,000	13.06%	
20			1989	$233,796	$1,400,000	14.31%	
21			1990	$320,268	$1,500,000	17.59%	

Test the buttons

You've set up buttons to run the macros. Run each macro by clicking its button.

1   Click the Update button.

2   Choose the Close button in the data form.

3   Click the Print button.

4   Choose the Close button in the print preview window.

Save your work

1   Choose File Save to save the worksheet.

2   Switch to the SALES MACRO macro sheet.

3   Choose File Save.

You Try It

You've just created macros to update a worksheet and view it in print preview. Now, you'll create a macro that plots the database in the WCS SALES worksheet in a chart. Then you'll create a button to run the macro.

Once you've created the chart macro and assigned it to a worksheet button, you'll add 1993 company and industry revenues to the WCS SALES worksheet, plot the data in a chart, and preview the printed page by clicking the Print button.

1   In the SALES MACRO macro sheet, select cell B18 and set the macro recorder.

2   Start the macro recorder.

3   Switch to the WCS SALES worksheet.

4   Use the Formula Goto command to select the database.

5   Open the SALES CHART17 TEMPLATE.

6   Click the zoom box to enlarge the chart.

7   Stop the macro recorder.

8   Switch to the SALES MACRO sheet.

In the following illustration, the macro has comments and formatting added. Your macro may be slightly different depending on the location of the SALES CHART17 TEMPLATE in your folder. Use the illustration to add comments and formatting to your macro.

	A	B	C
1		COMMAND MACROS	
2			
3	Cell Names	Macro name or statement	Shortcut key/Comments
4		**Update**	**(u)**
5		STEP()	Calculate one function at a time
6		=ACTIVATE("WCS SALES")	Make sure the worksheet is active
7		=DATA.FORM()	Display data form
8		=RETURN()	End macro
9			
10		**Print**	**(p)**
11		=ACTIVATE("WCS SALES")	Make sure worksheet is active
12		=FORMULA.GOTO("Database")	Select area named "Database"
13		=SET.PRINT.AREA()	Set selection as print area
14		=PRINT.PREVIEW()	Print preview
15		=RETURN()	End macro
16			
17		**Chart**	**(c)**
18		=ACTIVATE("WCS SALES")	Make sure worksheet is active
19		=FORMULA.GOTO("Database")	Select area named "Database"
20		=OPEN("SALES CHART17 TEMPLATE")	Open the SALES CHART17 TEMPLATE
21		=FULL(TRUE)	Expand the chart window
22		=RETURN()	End macro
23			
24			

9   Use the Formula Define Name command to name the macro **Chart**

Your macro is a command macro. Type **c** as the shortcut key.

10   Add a button to the WCS SALES worksheet and assign the Chart macro to the button.

11   Click the Update button and enter the following new record in the data form:

In this field	Type
Year	7/1/1993
Company	552000
Industry	2200000

12 Click the Chart button to plot the data in a chart.

Your chart should look like this:

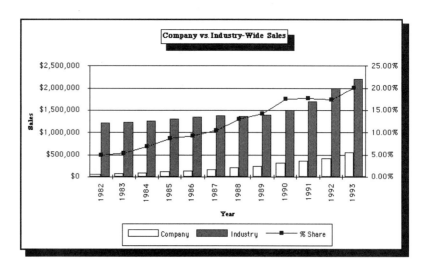

You've completed the WCS SALES worksheet. You can decide whether you want to save the chart. If you want to use the WCS SALES worksheet together with the SALES MACRO sheet, save the documents together as a workspace file. To see a solution to this exercise, open UTRYIT17 WORKSPACE. Close all the documents when you are finished.

Summary and Preview

In this lesson, you learned to:

Record a macro   You used the macro recorder to record macros that update, preview, and chart a worksheet database.

Understand a macro sheet   You learned how macro sheets are different from worksheets.

Edit and document a macro   You added and edited macro functions, formatted the macro sheet, and added comments explaining each formula.

Run a macro   You ran macros using the Macro Run command, the keyboard shortcut, and buttons.

Interrupt a macro   You learned how to use COMMAND+PERIOD or the ESC key to interrupt a macro.

Step through a macro   You used the STEP function to step through a macro one function at a time and to watch Microsoft Excel evaluate each part of the formula.

Assign macros to worksheet buttons   You used the button tool on the tool bar to create buttons; then you assigned macros to the buttons.

You have completed all the lessons in this tutorial. You now have the skills you need to use Microsoft Excel efficiently and productively. You can repeat any of the lessons at any time to brush up on specific Microsoft Excel features.

In the appendixes that follow, you can find out about converting files between Microsoft Excel and Lotus 1-2-3. You'll also find a list of new features in Microsoft Excel version 3.0 and a list of books that you might find helpful as you continue to learn Microsoft Excel.

Appendixes

Converting Lotus 1-2-3 Worksheets and Graphs

This appendix describes how to convert your worksheets between Lotus 1-2-3 and Microsoft Excel. You use the File Open command to open a 1-2-3 worksheet in Microsoft Excel. You use the File Save As command to save a Microsoft Excel worksheet in a 1-2-3 file format.

When you open a 1-2-3 worksheet in Microsoft Excel, your defined graphs are automatically converted into separate chart documents. You can't convert Microsoft Excel charts into 1-2-3 graphs.

For more information on converting your Lotus 1-2-3 worksheets and graphs, see Chapter 2, "Using Lotus 1-2-3 with Microsoft Excel," in the *Microsoft Excel User's Guide.*

Saving a Microsoft Excel Worksheet as a 1-2-3 Worksheet

To export a Microsoft Excel worksheet to another spreadsheet application, you save it in a different file format. Depending on the file format, you may lose some Microsoft Excel formatting.

The File Save As command   You use the File Save As command to save a document in a different file format. In the File Save As dialog box, choose the Options button to expand the dialog box and display the file format options. Select the appropriate file format option as listed in the following table.

To save a worksheet in this Lotus 1-2-3 format	Select this option
Release 1A format	WKS
Release 2 format	WK1
Release 3 format	WK3

Opening a 1-2-3 Worksheet in Microsoft Excel

To import data from a file created in another program into a Microsoft Excel worksheet, just open the file.

Microsoft Excel has options in the File Open and File Save As dialog boxes to translate file formats automatically.

The File Open command With File Open, you can open a file from a disk. Microsoft Excel automatically reads any of the file formats you can select in the File Save As dialog box.

- Normal
- Template
- Excel 2.2
- SYLK
- Text (ASCII)
- CSV

- WKS
- WK1
- WK3
- DIF
- DBF 2
- DBF 3

- DBF 4
- Text (Macintosh)
- Text (OS/2 or DOS)
- CSV (Macintosh)
- CSV (OS/2 or DOS)

Worksheet characteristics such as column width, label alignment, formulas, and most number formats can be converted between Microsoft Excel and 1-2-3. Borders, font formats, custom number formats, and worksheet objects are not converted into Lotus 1-2-3, because they don't exist in 1-2-3.

Saving a 1-2-3 Worksheet as a Microsoft Excel Worksheet

You can open a 1-2-3 worksheet with the Microsoft Excel File Open command, but it will retain its original file format until you save it in another file format. To change the worksheet into Microsoft Excel format, choose the File Save As command, choose the Options button, and select the Normal file format option.

Converting 1-2-3 Graphs to Microsoft Excel Charts

When you open a 1-2-3 worksheet that has graphs in Microsoft Excel, you see this message:

Because you can store many graphs on a single worksheet in 1-2-3, you should make sure you don't have so many graphs that you run out of memory when Microsoft Excel tries to create a separate window for each converted chart. Preparing your worksheets in 1-2-3 before you open them in Microsoft Excel can make the conversion smoother.

New Features of Microsoft Excel Version 3.0

The following tables list the features that are new in Microsoft Excel version 3.0, along with the lesson in this book in which you can learn about each feature. For features not described in this book, the appropriate chapter in the *Microsoft Excel User's Guide* is listed.

New Worksheet Features

To learn how to	See
Create charts directly on worksheets	Lesson 13, "Creating a Chart"
Draw graphic objects (lines, rectangles, ovals, and arcs) on worksheets	Lesson 16, "Using Embedded Charts and Worksheet Graphics"
Paste graphic objects onto worksheets	Lesson 16, "Using Embedded Charts and Worksheet Graphics"
Use the tool bar to draw, format, and apply styles on your worksheet	Lesson 3, "Formatting a Worksheet"
	Lesson 16, "Using Embedded Charts and Worksheet Graphics"
Type your comments in text boxes which you can move and size on the worksheet	Lesson 16, "Using Embedded Charts and Worksheet Graphics"
Outline your worksheet to organize your data into hierarchical levels	Lesson 7, "Worksheet Outlining and Data Consolidation"
Consolidate information from multiple worksheets into one worksheet	Lesson 7, "Worksheet Outlining and Data Consolidation"
Define documents as templates to reuse formatting, formulas, numbers, and text	Lesson 14, "Formatting a Chart"
Adjust margins and page setup settings from print preview	Lesson 10, "Setting Up the Page and Printing"
Embed objects from other applications into Microsoft Excel documents	*Microsoft Excel User's Guide*, Chapter 8, "Working with Data from Multiple Documents"
Edit a group of worksheets simultaneously	Lesson 7, "Worksheet Outlining and Data Consolidation"

To learn how to	See
Click a button on the tool bar to automatically sum a range	Lesson 2, "Creating a Worksheet" Lesson 8, "Advanced Worksheet Features"
Format cells with new colors, patterns, shading, and borders	Lesson 3, "Formatting a Worksheet"
Group formatting selections into cell styles, which you can apply to other worksheet selections	Lesson 3, "Formatting a Worksheet"
Use the Formula Goal Seek command to find a specific value that returns a specific result	Lesson 8, "Advanced Worksheet Features"
Assign a macro to a button or other object on a worksheet so that the macro runs when the object is clicked	Lesson 17, "Recording Macros"
Include up to 6,500 elements in an array	Lesson 8, "Advanced Worksheet Features"

New Chart Features

To learn how to	See
Create 3-D charts	Lesson 13, "Creating a Chart"
Use graphics as data series markers to create picture charts	Lesson 16, "Using Embedded Charts and Worksheet Graphics"
Create charts directly on worksheets	Lesson 13, "Creating a Chart"
Edit data series more easily	Lesson 15, "Editing Chart Data Series"
Drag data points to change the underlying worksheet data	*Microsoft Excel User's Guide,* Chapter 12, "Editing a Chart"
Format single data points in charts that include multiple series	*Microsoft Excel User's Guide,* Chapter 12, "Editing a Chart"
Place legends anywhere on a chart	Lesson 14, "Formatting a Chart"
Include up to 4,000 data points per data series	*Microsoft Excel User's Guide,* Chapter 12, "Editing a Chart"

New Macro Sheet Features

To learn how to	See in the *Microsoft Excel User's Guide*
Create updatable user-defined dialog boxes with drop-down lists and dynamic and dimmed items	Chapter 20, "Creating a Custom Application"
Use hidden names with automatic macros	Chapter 20, "Creating a Custom Application"
Create add-in macro sheets that are opened automatically when you start Microsoft Excel	Chapter 20, "Creating a Custom Application"
Create international macro sheets	Chapter 20, "Creating a Custom Application"
Create custom Undo and Repeat commands	Chapter 20, "Creating a Custom Application"
Use external code resources more easily	Chapter 20, "Creating a Custom Application"
Step through macros from the Macro Run dialog box	Chapter 19, "Designing and Writing a Command Macro"
Use the Goto button when a macro error occurs	Chapter 19, "Designing and Writing a Command Macro"
See functions as they are evaluated using the Evaluate button in the Single Step dialog box	Chapter 19, "Designing and Writing a Command Macro"

For More Information

For detailed information on spreadsheet design, see the following book:

Nevison, John M. *Microsoft Excel Spreadsheet Design*. New York, NY: Simon and Schuster, 1990.

For more information on displaying information graphically, see the following books:

Tufte, Edward R. *Envisioning Information*. Cheshire, CT: Graphics Press, 1990.

Tufte, Edward R. *The Visual Display of Quantitative Information*. Cheshire, CT: Graphics Press, 1983.

For more information on using Microsoft Excel, see the following books:

Alves, Jeffrey R., Bill Fletcher, and Dennis P. Curtin. *Planning and Budgeting with Excel*. Berkeley, CA: Osborne McGraw-Hill, 1986.

Hixson, Amanda C. *Advanced Excel for the PC*. Berkeley, CA: Osborne McGraw-Hill, 1988.

Kinata, Chris and Charles Kyd. *The Complete Guide to Microsoft Excel Macros*. Redmond, WA: Microsoft Press, 1991.

Kyd, Charles W. *Microsoft Excel Business Sourcebook*. Redmond, WA: Microsoft Press, 1988.

Nelson, Stephen L. *Microsoft Excel Money Manager*. Redmond, WA: Microsoft Press, 1989.

Nelson, Stephen L. *Microsoft Excel Small Business Consultant*. Redmond, WA: Microsoft Press, 1989.

Salkind, Neil J. *Excel: A Business User's Guide*. New York, NY: John Wiley & Sons, Inc., 1989.

Schieve, Paul L. and Jon I. Young. *Illustrated Microsoft Excel 2.10*. Plano, TX: Wordware Publishing, Inc., 1989.

The Cobb Group: Douglas Cobb and Allan McGuffey with Mark Dodge. *Microsoft Excel 3 Companion*. Redmond, WA: Microsoft Press, 1991.

The Cobb Group with Allan McGuffey. *Excel in Business*. Redmond, WA: Microsoft Press, 1989.

The Cobb Group with Craig Stinson. *Running Microsoft Excel,* 2nd edition. Redmond, WA: Microsoft Press, 1991.

Index

G

OTHER TITLES FROM MICROSOFT PRESS

MICROSOFT® EXCEL 3 COMPANION
Macintosh® Edition
The Cobb Group: Douglas Cobb and Allan McGuffey with Mark Dodge
"The definitive guide to Excel on the Macintosh. An outstanding reference for its readability and detail." **Computer Book Review**

Updated to cover version 3 of Microsoft Excel, MICROSOFT EXCEL 3 COMPANION has more than 900 pages of explanations, instruction, examples, and advice that make this the most comprehensive Microsoft Excel tutorial and reference book available. Whether you're a new user, occasional user, or power user, this book has the answers to all your Excel questions. Includes information on creating 3-D charts, using Microsoft Excel with System 7, developing ready-to-use spreadsheet templates, and much more.

912 pages $27.95   Order Code EX3CO

THE BIG BOOK OF AMAZING MAC® FACTS
Lon Poole

A superb collection of hundreds of useful tidbits from the author's "Quick Tips" column in *Macworld* magazine as well as from user groups and hardware and software manufacturers. This great collection is guaranteed to help you get the most out of your Macintosh—whether it's an older model or a new Classic, LC, or IIsi. Tips cover System 7 software and applications of all types—word processing, spreadsheets, graphics, communications, and desktop publishing.

528 pages $24.95   Order Code BIBOAM

MICROSOFT® WORD FOR THE APPLE® MACINTOSH®
Michael Boom

For those new to word processing or to Microsoft Word for the Apple Macintosh, this is the perfect starting point. The clear instruction and practical examples are designed to make the learning easy. Become productive immediately by following the step-by-step tutorials and examples to produce a letter, report, proposal, or newsletter. Covers version 4.

464 pages $19.95   Order Code WDAPMA

WORD 4 COMPANION
Macintosh® Edition
The Cobb Group: Gena B. Cobb, Allan McGuffey, and Judy Mynhier

A comprehensive guide, packed with easy-to-follow instructions and practical examples on Microsoft Word for the Apple Macintosh, version 4. This up-to-date tutorial and reference is for Word users at all levels. Beginners will appreciate the clear tutorials; intermediate and advanced users will value this book for its in depth information. Packed with hundreds of illustrations, practical examples, and special techniques for working with Word's menus.

864 pages $22.95   Order Code WO4CO

*To order call **1-800-MSPRESS** or use the order form on the next page.*

WORKING WITH WORD, 2nd ed.

Chris Kinata and Gordon McComb

*"The best book for getting inside Microsoft's word processor.
Geared for users of all levels."* **MacWeek**

The definitive guide to Microsoft Word for the Apple Macintosh through version 4.
This book is packed with timesaving tips for intermediate to advanced users. Every
feature of Microsoft Word is explained and explored. Detailed summaries at the end
of each chapter recap the main concepts with concise explanations. Includes step-by-
step instructions for creating newsletters, brochures, reports, and correspondence.

752 pages $22.95   Order Code WOWO2

DESKTOP PUBLISHING BY DESIGN, 2nd ed.
Aldus® PageMaker® edition

Ronnie Shushan and Don Wright

*"One of the most useful and attractive books we have seen on desktop
publishing and design....Full of ideas and inspiration."* **The New York Times**

Voted "Best How-to Book of 1990" by the Computer Press Association, DESKTOP
PUBLISHING BY DESIGN is the most fact-filled, design-oriented resource on Aldus
PageMaker version 4 for the Apple Macintosh and Windows 3 you'll find. Really three
books in one, DESKTOP PUBLISHING BY DESIGN is a primer on layout and design,
a portfolio of successful PageMaker designs, and a collection of hands-on projects.

416 pages $29.95   Order Code DEPUD2

ORDER FORM

Microsoft Press books are available wherever quality computer books are sold.

CORPORATE ORDERS

If you're placing a large-volume corporate order
for additional copies of
MICROSOFT® EXCEL STEP BY STEP
or any other Microsoft Press title,

you may be eligible for our corporate discount.

Instructor's Kit

Call for more information on the
Microsoft Excel Step by Step Instructor's Kit.

Call
1-800-888-3303, ext. 63460
for details.